PSYCHOSOCI[illegible] SS OF WOMEN TEA[illegible])LS

MW01674316

Chhabi Lata Dei

TABLE OF CONTENTS

LIST OF TABLES

LIST OF FIGURES

student-teacher interaction and collaboration that is flexible, democratic and person-centered. Now-a-days, teachers are supposed to be better recognized as facilitators than teaching experts. Further, Virtual tools and networking are opening borderless learning territories for students of all age groups, anytime and anywhere which require psychosocially and emotionally competent and well-prepared teachers to synthesize a multitude of tools for teaching and learning; co-mingling texts, images, audio, video, simulations, and games in reflective ways to re-wire students' development and use of knowledge. All these would require not only intellectually brilliant teachers but also psychosocially and emotionally competent ones.

Teachers of the 21st century are supposed to make countless complex decisions each day, often in varying contexts, with students of increasingly diverse nature and characters. Hence, new tools must be developed to identify effective teachers, and the educationists should not be guided by only relying on standardized academic test results as a means to determine who would be effective teachers. Many researchers have suggested that the best possible guidance for the recruitment of effective teachers is including the evaluation of psychosocial and emotional competence of teachers in the selection process of teacher recruitment.

For example, the Teach for America (TFA) corps in 2010, recruited 4000 teachers selecting them on psychosocial and emotional competence along with the criteria of academic competence. They taught students for a few years before they move on to more ambitious or lucrative careers. These teachers were engaged in some identified high-need schools, where students have different difficulties in their processes of life and learning, and most of them were demotivated for study. These three years of Head Start Program had in fact brought much-needed energy and enthusiasm among the students by the time the program was closed. It was found that during this period, the academic performance, behavior, attitude, socio-emotional maturity, competence, interpersonal skills, and even motivation and enthusiasm of students have improved in the range of 41% to 68% on the average for different abilities (Berry, Daughtrey, &Wieder, 2016). Hence, the study clearly suggested that teacher effectiveness has to be the primary concern of the social and educational scientists including the administration, who should look forward to the socio-emotional competence among the teachers.

Defining Teacher Effectiveness

Students are most affected by the quality of their teachers. They interact with teachers every day in the classroom, and the quality of that interaction matters a lot so far as their future development is concerned. But students are rarely asked what they think about a great teacher. Peterson (2015) carried out a survey research on 14 thousand students in the age group of 15-19 years across the United States about what they think of making an effective teacher. The top five qualities of a great teacher as accorded by those students were:

(i) ***The ability to develop relationships with their students-*** The most frequent response contributed by the students was that a great teacher builds trusting relationships with students in order to create a safe, positive, and productive learning environment. For example, a student in Boston told that great teachers are "Willing to listen to students when there is a problem." Several studies have reported about the teachers' listening characteristics as a major source of trusting relationships with students (e.g., Fitch & Adele, 2007; Wolvin, 2010).

(ii) ***Patient, caring, and kind personality-***Being compassionate and having sensitivity to student differences was found to be the second most frequently reported quality of an effective teacher. For example, some students reported that a caring teacher creates a positive atmosphere in the classroom that enhances their relationship with students and makes them feel important. A student is far more responsive to a teacher who cares, and is therefore more likely to learn and remain engaged in his /her class. There are also researches to support that teachers' dispositions are strongly related to student learning and development (e.g., Deiro, 1996; Palmer, 2011; Spark &Lipka, 1992).

(iii) ***Knowledge of learners-*** This is a broad category that incorporates knowledge of the teacher about cognitive, social and emotional development of the students. It includes an understanding of how students learn at a given developmental level; how learning in a specific subject area typically progresses; awareness that learners have individual needs and abilities; and an understanding that instruction should be tailored to meet each learner's needs. One student eloquently described it as: "The teacher understands the pace and capacity of the student". Evidences from research strongly supported that Teachers require knowledge of the unique skills that each child brings to the classroom in order to effectively target instruction towards students' learning needs (e. g., Brown & McIntyre, 2011; Elbaz, 2007; Kagan & Tippins, 2001).

(iv) ***Dedication to teaching-*** Dedication refers to the love for teaching or passion for the work, which includes commitment to students' success. Responses often referred to loving the subject matter or simply being dedicated to the work. To a student, this means a teacher should be "always willing to help and give time." There are innumerable evidences from research that passionate teachers create an effective learning environment and increase the learning potential of the students. Passionate teachers are committed and dedicated to their schools and a good educational achievement is an outcome of this commitment and dedication of the teacher. There are numerous studies in the research literature which claim the advantages of a dedicated teacher (e.g., Carbonneau, Vallerand, Fernet & Guay, 2008; Garrison & Liston, 2004; Hargreaves, 2012).

(v) ***Engaging students in learning***-Students also said that teachers should be able to engage and motivate students to learn. Researchers talk about three types of engagement that are required for students to learn: cognitive, emotional, and behavioral. Survey respondents mostly focused on making content interesting and the ability to motivate students to learn. A student in Pennsylvania said great teachers are, "motivating students to succeed in and out of school."There are strong evidences from research literature that while motivating students can be a difficult task, the rewards are more than worth it. Motivated students are more excited to learn and participate and teaching a class of motivated students is enjoyable for teacher and student alike (e.g., Bernaus, Wilson, & Gardner, 2009; Bruinsma, & Jansen, 2010; Butler, 2012).

The findings of the above survey research clearly pointed to the significance of teacher effectiveness in the changing paradigm and pedagogy of the learners of the 21st century. Therefore, the present research aiming at the study of teacher effectiveness, has derived its origin from the study of Walker (2008) who carried out a longitudinal study for fifteen years to identify the measurable factors of teacher effectiveness. He had engaged college students in discussions and writing assignments that pertain to the outstanding characteristics of their most effective teachers; "effective" meaning that these teachers made the most significant impact on their lives. Over the years 5400 students participated in the program. Based on those recurring themes, the conclusion was that effective teachers share at least ten clear characteristics, which consistently affected students in positive ways. Those characteristics as reported by Walker are described below.

Elaboration of Walker's Construct of Teacher Effectiveness

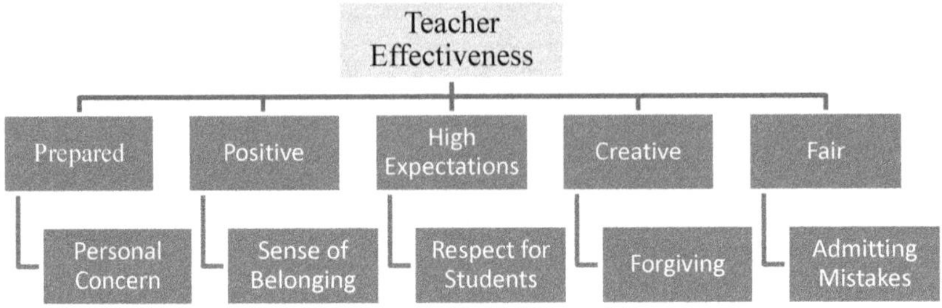

(1) Prepared: The most effective teachers come to class each day ready to teach.

i. It is easy to learn in their classes because they are ready for the day.
ii. They don't waste instructional time. They start class on time. They teach for the entire class period.
iii. Time flies in their classes because students are engaged in learning i.e., not bored, less likely to fall asleep.

(2) Positive: The most effective teachers have optimistic attitudes about teaching and about students.

i. They look on the positive side of every situation.
ii. They make themselves available to students.
iii. They communicate with students about their progress.
iv. They give praise and recognition.

v. They have strategies to help students act positively toward one another

(3) ***Hold High Expectations:*** The most effective teachers set no limits on students and believe everyone can be successful.

i. They hold the highest standards.
ii. They consistently challenge their students to do their best.
iii. They build students' confidence and teach them to believe in themselves.

(4) ***Creative:*** The most effective teachers are resourceful and inventive in how they teach in their classes.

i. The creative teachers have the ability to infuse lessons with meaning and purpose for their students.
ii. The creative teachers think outside the box and foster a love of learning in their students.
iii. Flexibility is both an attitude and a mindset of a creative teacher.
iv. Creative teachers still love to learn themselves.

(5) ***Fair**:* The most effective teachers handle students and grade them fairly.

i. They allow all students equal opportunities and privileges.
ii. They provide clear requirements for the class.
iii. They recognize that "fair" doesn't necessarily mean treating everyone the same but means giving every student an opportunity to succeed.

iv. They understand that not all students learn in the same way and at the same rate.

(6)***Display a Personal Touch:*** The most effective teachers are approachable.

i. They connect with students personally.
ii. They share personal experiences with their classes.
iii. They take personal interest in students and find out as much as possible about them.
iv. They visit the students' world (sit with them in the cafeteria; attend sporting events, plays, and other events outside normal school hours).

(7)***Cultivate a Sense of Belonging*:** The most effective teachers have a way of making students feel welcome and comfortable in their classrooms.

i. Students repeatedly mention that they felt as though they belonged in classrooms taught by effective teachers.
ii. The students knew they had a good teacher who loved teaching and preferred it to other occupations.

(8)***Respect for Students****:* The most effective teachers do not deliberately embarrass students. Teachers, who give the highest respect, get the highest respect.

i. They respect students' privacy when discussing about them.
ii. They speak to students in private concerning grades, conduct or behavior.

iii. They show sensitivity to feelings and consistently avoid situations that unnecessarily embarrass students.

***(9) Forgiving**:* The most effective teachers do not hold grudges.

i. They forgive students for inappropriate behavior.

ii. They habitually start each day with a clean slate.

iii. They understand that a forgiving attitude is essential to reaching difficult students.

iv. They understand that disruptive or antisocial behavior can quickly turn a teacher against a student, but that refusing to give up on difficult students can produce success.

*(10) **Admit Mistakes:*** The most effective teachers are quick to admit being wrong.

i. They apologize to mistakenly accused students.

ii. They make adjustments when students point out errors in grading or test material that has not been assigned.

The characteristics of effectiveness described above have many things to relate to the personality and socio-emotional characteristics of the teachers. These characteristics of teachers are not to be assumed as universal because any teacher is a cross product of socio-cultural perspectives where he or she lives. Hence, the matter of teacher effectiveness needs to be examined in any defined cultural context to provide the best benefit of the research to the community of students in their socio-cultural perspectives. In this context, the present research is planned to examine the psychosocial attributes of women primary teachers in Odisha and thereby highlight on their teacher effectiveness. The logic of having women primary teachers in the study would be explained in the later section.

Psychosocial Attributes

The idea of psychosocial attributes for the study was based on the contribution of Chatopadhyay (2014) who developed a battery of test to assess the socio-emotional competence of teachers in the Indian context which she designated as Psychosocial Attribute Measurement Battery (PAMB). The battery consisted of 10 different measures to assess the psychosocial attributes of teachers. The following are the elaboration of the constructs of Chatopadhyay's Scale to measure the psychosocial attributes of teachers. The scale was standardized in the context of teachers in the government primary to high schools in some states of India. Research studies were also carried out which reported on the substantial validity of the scale.

Chatopadhyay's Constructs of Effective Teachers' Psychosocial Attributes

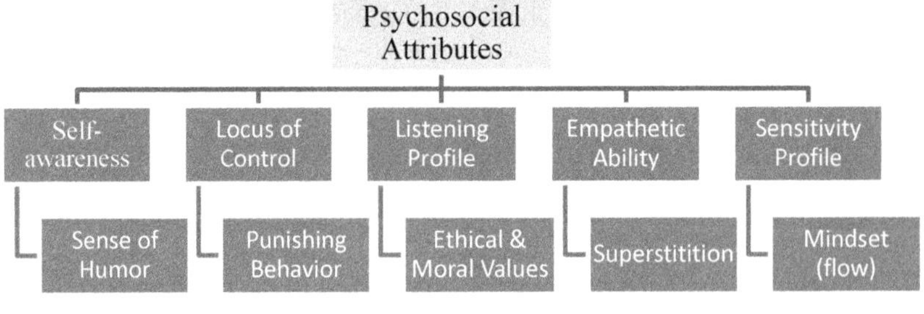

(i) Self-awareness is having a clear perception of one's personality, including strengths, weaknesses, thoughts, beliefs, motivation, and emotions. The hallmark of the self-aware teachers lies in catering to the diverse learning style, pace, culture, and mindsets of students (Larrivee, 2004; Richardson &Shupe, 2003). Self-awareness of teachers allows for better inter-personal synergies and enhances the interactions that are a crucial component of teaching. Self- awareness can be called as their intra-personal intelligence. A self-aware teacher will do well to know his or her core strengths and competencies as well as weaknesses with a view to devising teaching-learning strategies that compensate for those weaknesses. Developing self-awareness in teaching leads to transformative outcomes in student's skill acquisition (Hammond, 2007).

(ii) Locus of Control refers to the extent to which individuals believe that they can control the events affecting them. Teachers with high internal locus of control believe that students behavior in the school result primarily from their own behavior and actions. Several studies which investigated the relationships between teachers' locus of control and students' behavior and achievement (e.g., Findley & Cooper, 1983; Munir & Sazid, 2010; Rose & Medway, 1993) reported that teachers' internal locus of control not only help students for better academic achievement but also enhance their level of motivation and involvement in study.

(iii) Listening Profile. Human communication involves much more than words. Listening is more than having good communication skills. It is about having an attitude, and general spirit of honoring and seeking another person's perspective and a genuine interest in getting to know them. Studies have reported that teachers' listening profile is one of the most significant sources of students' good feeling, positive attitude towards study, attachment with school, and disciplined and emotional behavior (Hafen et al., 2015; Hill et al., 2015; Rockoff & Speroni, 2010). Above researchers have clearly emphasized that teachers who patiently listen to students, attend to and solve their problems are appreciated to be very effective teachers.

(iv) Empathetic Ability. Empathy is the ability to accurately put you in someone else's shoes; to understand the other's situation, perceptions and feelings from their point of view and to be able to communicate that understanding back to the other person. Empathy is a critical skill for successful teachers. Teacher-empathy is the ability to express concern and take the perspective of a student. Students' positive perception of their teachers' empathy has been found to influence their academic motivation (Branwhite, 2009) and has also been found to develop empathy among students (Hoffman, 2000). Gerstein (2012) in a study of contributions teachers' empathy on student's development described the following benefits of teachers' empathy to teaching, learning and classroom environment.

(i) It builds the foundation of the teacher-student relationship as the students feel that the teacher has a genuine interest in them and really understands them. (ii) Teachers' empathy best helps in the individualized, differentiated, and personalized education in the classroom. (iii) Teachers' empathy addresses the host of unmet social and emotional needs that students carry into the classroom as they demand that teachers be able to look below the surface and understand what's driving their particular set of behavior. (iv) Finally, when teachers demonstrate empathy, students see empathy in action and develop those skills for them.

(v) Sensitivity Profile. The sensitivity profile in the context of the present research particularly means the cultural sensitivity of the teachers. A culturally-sensitive teacher is one who is aware of and addresses the students' cultural and ethnic needs in order to obtain the students' cooperation. Irving and Hudley (2008) on a study of African students reported that presence of cultural mistrust and oppositional cultural attitudes in the student-teacher relationship clearly undermined the educational outcome of the students. On the other hand, cultural sensitivity among the teachers relating to the student's culture promoted strong cultural identity among students and positively influenced their academic performance. Altugan (2015) examined the relationship between cultural identity and learning process among some tribal students and reported that tribal students studying in residential schools where teachers were engaged from other communities face difficulties in learning and have poor academic performance compared to their counterparts who are taught in their own cultural setting by native teachers.

Altugan pointed out that an effective teacher needs to be culturally sensitive and responsive. According to him, culturally sensitive teachers need to purposefully respond to the needs of the many culturally and ethnically diverse students in their classrooms. Culturally responsive teaching includes implementing specifically student-oriented instructional processes as well as choosing and delivering ethnically and culturally relevant curricula. Culturally sensitive teachers use effective communication which may include translations to students' languages, and the use of teaching aids relevant to culture of the students. Culturally responsive teaching should include activities of the teacher that reflect the students' values, cultures, and beliefs.

(vi) Sense of Humor: A sense of humor is a positive personality trait and a sign of psychological strength. Along with gratitude, hope and spirituality, a sense of humor belongs to the set of strengths which positive psychologists called transcendence; together they help us forge connections to the world and provide meaning to life. Sense of humor is a significant teacher personality characteristic. Evidence indicates that teachers' sense of humor is related positively to increasing learners' intrinsic motivation which is resulting in better academic achievements (Rinninger, 2000). The use of humor to facilitate learning is not a new concept. It seems to be an emergence today as more teachers and educators look for methods to better communicate and help students learn. According to Dieter (2000) study on, "Teachers' sense of humor on Students learning", sense of humor is one instructional tool that teachers can use in the classroom to increase their effectiveness. All the participants in the study agreed that teacher's sense of humor made their classes more interesting and comfortable, and helped them to be more confident about their learning.

According Makewa et al., (2011), the use of humor in teaching attract the attention of students, motivate them very well reducing their anxiety in the classroom and stimulate their minds. The use of humor is good and effective in continuous learning strategy as it enhances the understanding of content, increases retention of material being taught, and creates a more comfortable learning environment (Makewa, Role, & Genga, 2011). Results of research on the integration of humor in the teaching of Mathematics also reported that humor can make a fun atmosphere in the class reducing anxiety, increasing motivation and interest in learning Mathematics, and it also increases creativity (Gazit, 2013).

(vii) Punishing Behavior: In psychology, punishment is defined as addition of an aversive stimulus or removal of a pleasant stimulus. Many teachers use this method to manage and control students' learning and behavior in the classroom. Even though these practices are widely used, many educators question them as good teaching practices. The effectiveness of punishment versus reward in classroom is an ongoing issue for education professionals. Both tactics provide teachers with leverage when dealing with disruptive and self-motivated students.

Bandura (1973) suggested that, physical punishment make children to learn aggressive behavior through modeling. If teachers try to modify students' behavior through inflicting pain, then those students are likely to do the same to others when they want to influence other people's actions. Socio-cultural and cognitive theorists also insist that, punishment may legitimize violence in students' interpersonal relationships because they tend to internalize the social relation they experience (Kail, 2006). Deiro (1996) reported from his study on student's perception of punishing teachers that majority of students perceive their punishing teacher as bad and fearful and they try to keep away from them. They said that they don't like to attend the classes of those teachers who give physical punishments and most of them do not believe that they are good teachers.

(viii) Ethical and Moral Values: The core of teaching consists of four basic values: dignity, truthfulness, fairness and responsibility. All teaching is founded on ethics – whether it is the teacher-student relationship, or a teacher's relationship with his work. Tirri (2011) pointed out that students benefit both socially and academically from the teacher's moral behavior as well as from teacher's professional ethics and values. The participants of his study were 360 successful adults who were asked to remind of their best teachers and also to tell why they consider them as best. More than 70% of the contents in their responses reported about appreciation of ethical and moral values of their teachers. On the other hand, when asked about bad teachers they have come across, almost all of them pointed out some lack in ethical and moral values.

(ix) Superstition: Superstition is a pejorative term for any belief or practice that is considered irrational or supernatural. It arises from ignorance, a misunderstanding of science or causality, a positive belief in black magic, or fear of that which is unknown. Donald (2014) pointed out that teachers' superstition very strongly influence the students behavior in the classroom. In his study he identified 60 teachers from 10 different schools each of them having some strong peculiar superstitions. When he assessed the students' behavior in those schools relating to the superstitions, he found that the students have the same kind of superstitions as their teachers have. Josephine et al. (2015) from a study on students superstitious believes and academic performance pointed out that the academic performance of the students significantly decreased by superstitious beliefs in four categories of good luck, bad lock, impending danger, and perceived effect. They also pointed out that teachers who do not emphasize on those superstitions are found to have better student performance in their subjects of teaching.

(x) Flow Mindset: A flow mindset allows a person to approach life with curiosity and exuberance. The goal of a flow mindset is the attainment of peak experiences. In positive psychology, a flow is the mental state of operation in which a person performing an activity is fully immersed in a feeling of energized focus, full involvement, and enjoyment in the process of the activity.

Educational consultants working to support Developmental Design implementation in classrooms have noted that successful teachers work from three fundamental frames of mind: Growth or flow mind set referring to the space of possibilities that a teacher holds for each student, and teacher's believe in the students capacity for growth into responsible independence as they guide them; Action mind set referring to active support to each student through good times and bad which demand a commitment of heart and mind fueled by a sense of urgency; and Objective mind set referring to the ability to interact with students without taking what they do and say personally.

Palmer (1998) reported on the following characteristics of the flow mind set of the teachers:(i) everyone can grow and this simple but crucial belief builds power when applied to teaching; (ii) Some students need more guidance than others; (iii) Given plasticity of the brain students can grow new and positive habits any time; (iv) effort not talent is the best path to mastery; (v) Every teacher has the capacity to grow their skills so that all students' needs are addressed; and finally (vi) challenges, setbacks and criticisms are welcome, because they provide a context for growth. York (2014) assessing the impact of teachers flow mind set on students' performance reported that it helped the students to develop a positive relationships among them, they become more respectful to teachers, increased their endorsement to teachers and their motivation for learning, becoming strategic, and finally, to be more creative and productive in academic performance. York also reported that the influences of teachers become so loud that their socio-emotional and problem solving behaviors have also been positively boosted.

The above evidences drawn from the cross-cultural literature clearly pointed out that Chatopadhyaya's proposed psychosocial attributes are profound parameters to assess the teacher effectiveness. Hence, the present study used all these parameters to assess the effectiveness of women primary teachers in Odisha and thereby examine the state of affairs in primary education in Odisha.

Psychological Capital

Thanks to its founder Martin Seligman, in 1999 the new science of positive psychology emerged as a rescue to the troubled human beings. The aim of this science is to enhance self-efficacy of the individual, focus on how to exploit the strengths rather than on weaknesses, look for opportunities instead of looking for threats, and generally activate functional, efficient and holistic approach to life (Seligman, 2002). Under the banner of positive psychology, Luthanset. al., (2004) identified the dimensions of psychological capital (PsyCap) which is defined as the positive and developmental state of an individual characterized by high self-efficacy, optimism, hope and resiliency.

Concept Elaboration of PsyCap

H	E	R	O
Hope	**Self-Efficacy**	**Resilience**	**Optimism**
A sense of energy to preserve towards your goals through proactive planning	A belief in your own ability to produce positive results and achieve self-defined goals	A positive way of coping even when it seems that there are no solutions to negative situations	Being and remaining positive about the likelihood of personal success, now and in the future.

Hope: Hope is an important component of the PsyCap related with the physical and mental health and is the ability to deal with the trouble and distress. According to Peterson and Byron (2008) hope is positively associated with job performance, leadership, organizational commitment, job satisfaction, and work happiness. Harvey et al., (2007) found that hope comprised of three components like power, goals and path, which provides realism and challenge to achieve the goals. Hope is the ability to determine, illuminate and follow the best way to success. People with high levels of hope have the capacity to deal with all the situations. Luthans et al. (2007) argued that hopeful individuals have high energy to identify the goal and develop alternative pathways to attain these goals. It is also found that hopeful people are considered as independent thinkers. When all the ways are blocked, hopeful and dedicated individuals like to take risk and find different alternative pathways to success (Luthans, et. al., 2004).

Self-efficacy: Self-efficacy is an individual's belief in his or her innate ability to achieve goals. Albert Bandura defines it as a personal judgment of "how well one can execute courses of action required to deal with prospective situations". Self-efficacy beliefs determine how people feel, think, motivate themselves and behave. The sources of self-efficacy according to Goleman (2006) are mastery experiences, vicarious experiences, verbal persuasion, emotional and physiological states, and imaginal experiences. The individual development of self-efficacy beliefs has its roots in early contingency experiences, in the use of degrees of freedom, and in the experience of success and failure depending on appropriate causal attributions. These basic experiences also hint at the most effective educational and psychotherapeutic approaches.

Resilience: Third important component of psychological capital is resilience. According to Luthans et al. (2007) resilience is the capability of the individuals to strike back from uncertainty and failure. Masten and Wright (2010) referred to resilience as the process of positive arrangement and modification in difficult and tough environment. Individuals with high resilience have the ability to take risk and overcome the risk. They are optimistic, humorous, curious and energetic towards life. These individuals are innovative, like new experiences and use creative exploration. Kappagoda et al. (2014a) characterized resilience as "a positive force that might be utilized to counter the negative events by adding the extreme positive events". Enzi and Ibrahim (2012) stated the three basis of resilience as (Cs): connectedness, coherence, and control.

Optimism:The theory of optimism as a positive organizational behavior (POB) is originated by Seligman (2007). Optimism is characterized as making stable, global and internal attribution towards achievement of goals. According to Seligman (2007), optimists are those who anticipate that positive things will happen in life. But pessimists are those thinking about the negative things in life. Self-assured person has a feeling that the positive and constructive events and occasions happen as consequence of their own behavior and practices. Optimism is an activity that is related to achieve the target and self-regulation. So, optimist's sense positivity comes in reaction to their behavior and actions. Seligman (2007) stated that the individuals who have positive attitude towards incidents, an internal stability, global attribution and inward steadiness are optimists. Totterdell et al., (2006) found that the characteristics of stress are positively mediated by the optimism.

Simarasl et al. (2010) found that optimism is a broad or common belief that good events occur more than bad events in the future.

Researchers in the field of PsyCap became interested to study how to maximize investment in human resources, and the optimal use of human abilities in alleviating the problems that may be encountered by an individual in the work environment (Avey, et al., 2011).This outlook gained interest of many researchers in the management of human resources, because of its positive impact on many personal and organizational variables, such as productivity, motivation, performance, organizational commitment, and the quality of work life (Sin & Lyubomirsky, 2009; Mortazavi, et al., 2012 Etebarian, et al., 2012).During the past two decades, enormous researches have been carried out on the developmental characteristics of PsyCap and its functional significance on human activities, behavior and performance. Several studies have also reported on the significance of teachers' PsyCap on students' behavior, performance, and future orientation.

Work motivation is one of the most important constructs for teacher effectiveness. According to Jesus and Lens (2005) teacher motivation is a decisive factor for school success. Several studies (e.g., Santisi, Magnano, Hichy, &Ramaci, 2014) underlined that teacher motivation is crucial for student motivation and school functioning. A review of Jesus (2003), on this subject, evidenced that majority of studies did not present a solid theoretical approach and the main addressed topics were the salary and incentives. On the other hand, Addison and Brundrett (2008) argued that teachers' PsyCap have great influence on student motivation influencing the: (a) quality of teaching; (b) student performance; (c) class well-being; (d) improvement of students' self-efficacy beliefs; and (e) development of the teacher-student relationship. Santisi et al., (2014) from a study on primary school teachers, pointed out that teachers' PsyCap is a significant source of teacher effectiveness which contributed to an all-round appreciation of the teachers.

Wang, Chen & Hsu (2014) examined the relationship between psychological capital and teaching effectiveness of elementary school teachers. They observed highly significant positive correlations among the measures of teacher effectiveness such as philosophy of teaching, teaching strategy, teaching assessment, class leadership, and overall teaching effectiveness and the measures of PsyCap. Similarly, Ming, Chou, Chin, and Wu (2017) examined the relationship between PsyCap and professional commitment of teachers and reported that professional commitment in terms of affective commitment, continuance commitment and normative commitment are closely interlinked with the teachers' PsyCap. Several such studies have pointed out the importance of teachers' PsyCap on students' life. Hence, the present study trying to examine the effectiveness of women primary teachers has proposed to examine the state of affairs of their PsyCap and study the impact of their PsyCap on their effectiveness as teachers.

Chapter II

Review of Literature

This section presents an elaboration of the constructs relating to of teachers' psychosocial attributes, psychological capital, and teacher effectiveness. Selective review of research, inferences, and implications related to all the above aspects of teacher attributes and effectiveness are cited and discussed from Indian and cross-cultural research literature to develop a background and rationale for the present research. The citations are organized in three stages; (i) Research relating to factors of teacher effectiveness, (ii) Research relating to the factors of psychosocial attributes of teachers and (iii) Research relating to the psychological capital of the teachers. Finally, basing on the review of these prior studied, the objectives and hypotheses of the present study were formulated.

Teacher Effectiveness

For nearly half a century, teacher effectiveness and teacher quality have become the focus of attention in educational and psychological research. Several countries in the world are implementing diverse sets of strategies that aim to improve the quality of education by improving the quality of teachers. Researchers have shown that teacher effectiveness is one of the keys to improve students' socio-emotional and educational outcomes. Clotfelter, Ladd &Vigdor, (2007) found that effective teachers have significant impact on students' ability not only to learn but also to behave in desired ways and not only in the school context but also in the context of their future life. Gordon, Kane &Staiger (2006) also found that students, who consistently have effective teachers during primary to high school years, exponentially benefit from schooling both in academic and socio-emotional skills. Alliance for Excellent Education (2004) emphasized the fact that teacher effectiveness, more than any other indicator of teacher quality, is the area in which policy makers and educators must focus their attention in order to improve students' socio-emotional and educational achievement.

Since 1950s, teacher effectiveness has been a focus of educational and psychological research because of its importance and relevance in the students' achievement at school. Researches on teacher effectiveness have focused on various aspects ranging from indicators of teacher effectiveness to paradigms of operations and measurement. Johnson (1990) viewed teacher effectiveness as the extent to which the teacher does things, or behaves in ways that are favorable to the development of skills, work habits, understandings, desirable attitudes, and adequate personal adjustment on the part of the students. He defined the essence of a teacher's role as guiding the learning and development of students, and all other roles and responsibilities considered important in enhancing this essential function. Campbell, Kyriakides, Muijs& Robinson (2003) defined teacher effectiveness as the power delegated to students by the teacher for socially valued objectives including enabling pupils to learn.

Studies of Bajunid (2000), and Coopers, (2001) have also shown that the significance of teachers' work outside the classroom is also increasing, and that teachers typically spend less of their working time on classroom instruction, while spending more time on lesson preparation, evaluation, report writing, curriculum development, and social and welfare tasks of pupils and parents. Empirical studies of teachers' work by Campbell & Neill (1994) also showed that teachers typically spend less than half their working time on classroom instruction while the remaining time is occupied by other extra-classroom activities. It has also being postulated that given the education reforms and the development of modern education systems, the roles of the teacher should not be limited to cognitive activities; rather, they should include the management of students, relationships, and handling of welfare matters in the school system.

Clinton, Aston, and Koelle (2015) investigating the characteristics of effective teachers carried out a meta-analysis on 52 relevant studies and extensively reported on the relationships between variables of effective teachers and students' learning, and characteristics which are positively associated with student-teacher relationship. A total of nine characteristics were identified in the study. These characteristics include cognition, social and emotional competence, self-efficacy, communication, motivation, cultural competence, personality, self-reflection, and collegiality. Clinton et al. described the following characteristics of effective teachers and finally, provided a summary of their relationships to the outcome interest for both students and teachers with an explanatory model of the relationships.

Explaining Effective Teacher Characteristics

(i) Cognitive capability. This capacity included the teachers' ability for creativity, critical thinking, and competence.

(ii) Social and emotional competence. Socio-emotional competence of the teachers refers to the coordinating and organizing capacity of the teacher to develop a framework as to how the teachers, parents and families of the students, and communities grow in partnership to promote students' social, emotional, and academic learning. Clinton et al. (2015) have recognized five core socio-emotional competencies of the teachers as self-awareness, self-management, social awareness, relationship skills, and responsible decision-making.

(iii) Self-efficacy. Teacher efficacy is when a teacher believes in their own ability to guide their students to success. For over thirty years, researchers have explored the link between teacher self-efficacy and student achievement. Research suggests that teachers with a strong sense of self-efficacy tend to be better planners, more resilient through failure, and more open-minded and supportive with students. Collective efficacy is when a team of teachers believe that together they can inspire growth and change in their students. According Hattie (2015) collective teacher efficacy has the greatest impact on student achievement, even higher than factors like teacher-student relationships, home environment, or parental involvement.

(iv) Communication. Teachers' communication refers their act of transmitting information including verbal and non-verbal which includes their communication style, body language, paralanguage, appearance, and instructional communication. According to Clinton et al. (2015) effective teachers communicate concern and caring by their tone of voice and use of body language. They transmit genuine commitment and affection for their students. Good teachers care about their students' progress and let their students know it at all times. They learn their students' names early in the school year and use their names when addressing them. They get to know their students' hopes, fears and preferences and communicate this knowledge to their students. They communicate their appreciation for what their students do by celebrating their successes and constantly encouraging them. This helps students feel recognized and validated.

(v) Motivation. It refers to the drive of the teachers which influence their behavior. Teacher's motivating style toward students revolves around what they say and do during instruction to motivate students to engage in learning activities which manifests itself in terms of autonomy-supportive versus controlling teaching. According to Clinton et al. (2015) a teacher's own personal motivation resolves around the extent of psychological need satisfaction experienced during the act of teaching, and it manifests itself in terms of teacher enthusiasm and job satisfaction.

(vi) Cultural competence. Teachers' culture competence refers to the awareness of their own culture, awareness of the diversities in students' culture, their views on the diversities, and their ability to successfully teach students who identify with a culture or cultures other than their own. Salmona et al., (2015) in his paper on developing culturally competent teachers found that teachers are required to address learning from a cultural perspective and those who are lacking in the foundational knowledge of students' culture face strong alienations from students. He further observed that in order to be effective teachers, it demanded on them to be in a continuous process of acculturation and teachers who do not fulfill the criteria are ultimately rejected by the students. Beutel (2010) reported from a study that cultural competence of the teachers results in a student-teacher complimentary relationship which manifests in students all-round development.

(vii) Personality. The combination of characteristics or qualities that make up a good teacher is referred to as teacher personality. There are several models explaining teacher-personality all of which conclude that teacher-personality is a great source of teacher effectiveness. For example, Kim et al., (2018) studying the teacher personality and teacher effectiveness in secondary schools reported that students rated the teachers with more of a conscientious personality trait as more academically supportive, with an agreeable trait as more sympathetic and kind, with emotional stability trait as more expecting from students, with extraversion trait as more socially demanding, and with openness to experience trait as more realistic and practical. Hence, according to Clinton et al. (2015) teacher-personality is a very significant source of teacher effectiveness.

(viii) Self-reflection. It refers to the teacher's reflective processes in identifying own strengths and weaknesses in their teaching style and practice, and their ability to adapt or correct them accordingly. Noormohammodi (2014) explained that teacher's self reflection is his process of examining beliefs, goals and practices to improve student learning. The results of his study showed that there was positive relationship between teachers' reflective practice, teachers' self-efficacy and autonomy. He has also reported that students have more identification with teachers who involve self-reflection in their teaching process. Under such teachers, students become more diversified and flexible in their divergent thinking, academic and cognitive performance.

(ix) Collegiality. Collegiality defines the cooperative relationship between teachers and their colleagues in this context the collaborative work, and encouragement and optimization of peer relationship among the students. Shah (2012) observed from a study that teacher's collegiality plays a vital role in augmenting teacher professional growth, development, job satisfaction, organizational and professional commitment as well as school quality and student performance.

The following is the proposed explanatory relationships among teacher characteristics, students' outcome, teacher outcome and school outcome (Clinton, Aston, and Koelle, 2015)

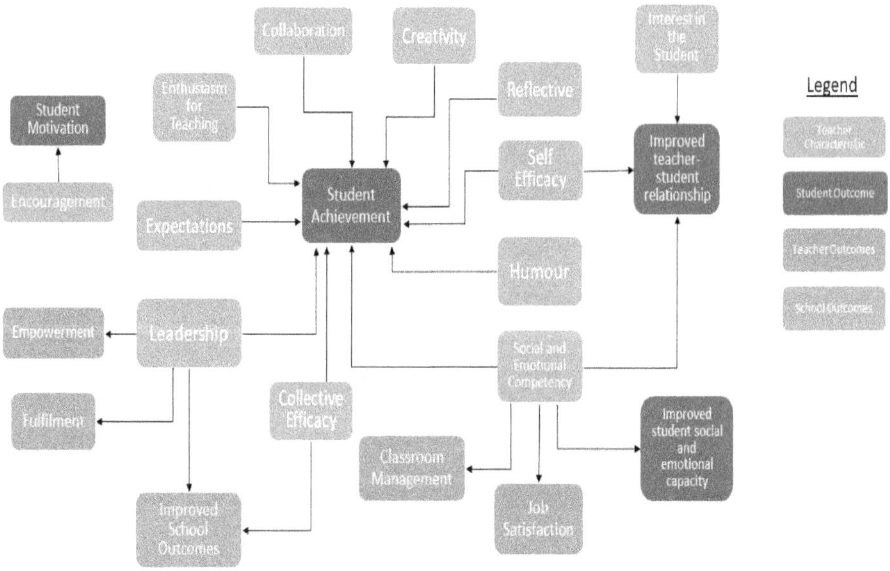

Measuring Teacher Effectiveness

Although various conceptualizations of teacher effectiveness have been proposed in the literature (e.g., Muijs, 2006), a consensual definition of teacher effectiveness has not been clearly outlined (e.g., Goe et al., 2008). In fact, recently Kane et al. (2008) have undertaken the project Measures of Effective Teaching (MET) which was designed to assess and promote effective teaching, and the study included three measures of teacher effectiveness: student evaluations of teaching, classroom observation, and student academic achievement.

Student evaluations of teaching aim to capture students' perception of the classroom and the teacher. Of many measures of student evaluations, the Tripod perception survey is the most popularly used tool (Wallace et al., 2016), which consists of seven dimensions, including care (level of interpersonal relationship support), confer (level of soliciting and inviting students' perspectives), and captivate (level of interest and relevancy of teaching). Tripod is adapted for two educational levels; elementary and secondary. In higher education, one of the most widely used student evaluation tools of teacher effectiveness is the Student Evaluations of Educational Quality questionnaire (SEEQ; Marsh, 1984), which contains seven domains assessing the level of teaching, including group interaction (stimulation of classroom discussions and enquiry), enthusiasm (level of enthusiasm in the classroom), and organization (clarity of instructions, preparation of course material). Some researchers argue the validity of student evaluations as a marker of student learning (e.g., Clayson 2009). However, its frequent use by practitioners and policymakers to provide feedback to instructors and make high-stake decisions (Glazerman et al. 2005) compels researchers to consider it as a good teacher effectiveness measure.

Classroom observations are one of the most intensive measures of teacher effectiveness. It often requires training the observers to code an individual's effectiveness in the classroom over multiple markers. The most common classroom observation tools are Classroom Assessment Scoring System (CLASS; Pianta et al. 2008) and Danielson's Framework for Teaching (Danielson, 2013), both of which were implemented in the study. CLASS offers an observation tool adapted for different educational levels (i.e., infant, toddler, lower elementary, upper elementary, and secondary), whereas Frame work for Teaching offers an observation adapted for different subject areas (i.e., mathematic and English Language Arts) as well as a generic subject area.

Student academic achievement, a marker for the level and progress of student learning, is arguably the most common measure of teacher effectiveness and is often considered as a gold standard outcome to evaluate the influences of various factors on teacher effectiveness. The type of achievement outcome used can vary, including standardized test scores, such as the Texas Assessment of Knowledge Skills test (e.g., Garcia et al. 2011), as well as non-standardized scores, such as school GPA or ACT scores and university subject marks (e.g., Kim and MacCann, 2018).

Student performance self-efficacy (PSE, also known as academic performance self-efficacy) is also a teacher effectiveness measure, which is students' perception of their capability to perform academically (Shell &Husman, 2001). With a strong theoretical background, within social cognitive theory (Bandura, 1986), PSE is mostly used in student non-cognitive research to understand its effect on student academic functioning and how it can be enhanced (e.g., Schunk & Ertmer, 2000). PSE is most often measured by asking students to report a mark that they expect to receive in a particular subject (e.g., Kim and MacCann 2018) or their confidence that they will perform well academically on specific tasks, such as note taking, test taking, and writing papers (e.g., Chemers et al. 2001). Each of the above-mentioned teacher effectiveness measures can contribute uniquely to provide a holistic picture of teacher effectiveness (Muijs, 2006; Rockoff & Speroni, 2010).

Teacher Personality and their Job-related Outcomes

Previous studies have examined the associations between teacher factors and teacher effectiveness. Some of the most notable teacher effectiveness findings are those from Hattie, who updated his original meta-analysis of meta-analyses (Hattie, 2015) to list over 250 factors that impact on student academic achievement. These factors are categorized into seven sources of impact: (a) teaching (teaching/instruction strategies, student learning strategies, and implementation methods), (b) teacher, (c) student, (d) school, (e) home, (f) curricula, and (g) classroom. The teacher source is further divided into teacher attributes, teacher-student interactions, and teacher education. Hattie (2009) observed that the strengths of the effect sizes vary among the 14 identified teaching and teacher factors, ranging from teacher performance ($d = .05$) to teacher estimates of student achievement ($d = 1.29$). Teacher personality is also included in the list of factors ($d = 0.24$). Klassen and Tze, (2014) carried out a meta-analysis between teacher personality and teacher effectiveness and found a significant relationship ($r = .28, p < .01$). However, like Hattie, they also considered teacher personality as a unidimensional construct, which is not in line with dominant personality theories, including the Big Five framework.

Arising from this limitation, Gorden (2017) studied the potential associations of each of the Big Five traits with teacher effectiveness. They have observed that teachers with high levels of conscientiousness tend to be achievement-focused, highly responsible, and organized. As such behaviors are helpful in successful completion of tasks; conscientiousness has been found as the strongest predictor of teacher effectiveness. Particularly, the facets of achievement striving (drive to achieve goals), dutifulness (sense of moral conscience), and self-discipline (ability to begin and complete tasks) are most positively associated with the effectiveness of the teachers.

Similarly, Klassen et al., (2014) identified that organization and planning were important personal characteristics for effective teachers. This group of characteristics captured the teachers' ability to manage competing priorities and their time, and display general organization skills, which are conceptually very similar to elements of conscientiousness, and thus indicating that conscientiousness may also be an important predictor of teacher effectiveness. Further, empirical findings also support that teacher conscientiousness is positively associated with teacher effectiveness measures (e.g., Garcia et al. 2011; Kim et al. 2018; Kim and MacCann 2018; Murray et al. 1990). For example, Patrick (2011) found that overall teacher effectiveness were predicted most strongly by high levels of teacher conscientiousness, even after controlling for students' previous learning and expected grade.

Likewise, John et al. (2008) reported that individuals with high levels of emotional stability are calm, secure, and tolerant of stress and these qualities are helpful to establish trust and credibility with others, particularly for jobs requiring interpersonal interactions. In appreciation of these findings, Gorden (2017) reported that emotional stability is the second strongest predictor of teacher effectiveness. Particularly, the facets of impulsiveness (low self-control), depression (guilt, sadness), and anxiety (fear, worry) are most negatively associated with teacher effectiveness. Frenzel et al. (2018) reported in a study that teachers are emotional contagions; their emotions displayed in the classroom can be transmitted to students. Students too become anxious and nervous, when observing an anxious and nervous teacher. In turn, students' perceptions of the school and the teachers affect their academic and socio-emotional ability.

Fielden et al. (2015) in a study reported that individuals with high levels of extraversion display their energy outwards, which is positively associated with higher levels of communication, sensitivity, disclosure, and provision of social support. Barrick and Mount (1991) found in their meta-analysis that extraversion was positively associated with job performance for occupational groups requiring interpersonal interactions. In the line of these findings, Gorden (2017) observed that teaching requires assertiveness and social interaction for which gregariousness and sociability may be an advantage. These are being the qualities of extraversion, they observed that teachers' extraversion is positively and strongly associated with their effectiveness as teachers.

John et al. (2008) reported in a study that individuals with high levels of agreeableness are kind, charming, caring, and helpful. Such qualities can be helpful to create positive and warm environments, which students require in learning. Gorden (2017) reported that agreeableness is also a very strong predictor of teacher effectiveness. Agreeableness conceptually aligned with empathy and communication was also identified as an effective teacher characteristic in Klassen et al.'s (2017) study. According to them, this quality measures the teacher's level of actively listening and engaging in a conversation, seeking advice, and adjusting their communication style. Findings from empirical study also supported the importance of agreeableness in students' perceptions of effective teaching. At primary level, teacher agreeableness was the strongest predictor of overall teacher evaluation, individual rapport, and enthusiasm (Kim and MacCann 2018). At secondary level, teacher agreeableness was the strongest predictor of students' report of teacher personal support (Kim et al. 2018). The quality of being warm and sensitive with students, staff, and parents is a quality required in teachers as they come to interact with them.

John et al. (2008) reported that individuals with high levels of openness are intellectually curious, creative, and liberal. Openness is one of the weakest predictors of job performance, although the values (readiness to reexamine opinions and values, liberal) facet of the domain still seems to be important in predicting job performance (Judge et al. 2013). Openness is also aligned with Klassen et al.'s (2017) adaptability aspect of the resilience and adaptability domain, which measures teacher's level of flexibility in lesson delivery and persistence. Patrick (2011) reported that teacher's openness was the strongest predictor of overall class ratings, controlling for students' previous learning and expected grade. Similarly, Kim and MacCann (2016) found that teacher openness was the strongest predictor of overall course evaluations. The ability to be flexible in teaching and engaging with students' ideas and opinions is a highly valued quality in teachers and a strong source of teacher effectiveness. The above discussions pointed out many of the teachers' personality variables as sources of his /her psychosocial attributes for teacher effectiveness. Some of those variables are included in the present study to examine the effectiveness of the women primary teachers in Odisha.

Review of Studies on Causal Factors of Teacher Effectiveness

Researchers during the past half century have focused on various causal factors of teacher effectiveness including gender, age, experience, training, educational status, personality characteristics, teaching aptitude, motivation and several other factors. The following is a chronological account of the studies relating causal factors to teacher effectiveness citing evidences from cross-cultural research and including many Indian studies. Sharma (1991) investigated the relationship between characteristics possessed by teachers and teacher effectiveness with a view to predicting teacher success. Working with 300 primary school teachers he observed that teaching aptitude appeared to be the strongest predictor of teacher effectiveness. Sharma defined teaching aptitude in terms of interest in teaching, orientation to teaching, implementing methods and principles of teaching, and teaching skill.

Chhaya (1974) investigated into certain psychological characteristics of an effective school teacher, which was conducted on 80 effective and 100 ineffective higher secondary teachers. The findings were that (i) effective teachers had significantly better adjustment and more favorable attitude towards teaching than ineffective teachers (ii) effective teachers showed significantly more interest in teaching than ineffective teachers, (iii) effective teachers were significantly more emotionally stable than ineffective teachers and (iv) effective teachers were more extrovert than ineffective teachers. Hence, the findings pointed to some important personality variables and teaching aptitude as sources of teacher effectiveness.

Kaul (1974) factor analyzed the personality traits of popular secondary teachers and arrived at four factors namely; striving, self-confidence, ability for perseverance, and calmness. In another factor analytical study on the intellectual and personality correlates of teacher effectiveness, Grewal (1976) found that the measures of personality traits such as locus of control, extroversion, sense of humor, listening ability, and flow mindset are criterion measures of teacher effectiveness. Some of these measures are used in the present study to assess the effectiveness of women teachers in Odisha.

Goel (1978) reported that extroversion is an important factor related to teacher effectiveness. Using the Flander's Interactive Analysis System, he found extrovert teachers to have greater interchange of classroom events than introvert teachers. The extrovert teachers provide a large range of behavior for pupils' responses in terms of praise, encouragement and questioning as compared to introvert teachers. It also appeared that extrovert teachers had all the seven interaction characteristics of critical teaching behavior such as composure, encouragement, assertiveness, choices, empathy, positive intent and consequentiality while introvert teachers had only first three interaction characteristics of teaching behavior. In conclusion, he said that the personality dimension of extraversion is important in shaping the teacher's behavior and consequently, the student's behavior and achievement.

Mutha's (1980) study attempted to identify the attitudinal, motivational and personality factors which differentiated effective teachers from ineffective teachers. The major findings of the study were that gender, professional training, and income levels of the teacher were significantly associated with the teacher effectiveness. Women teachers are more effective in primary classes, while men are more effective in high school and higher secondary classes. He has also further reported that women teachers are more effective in teaching language and social science subjects, while men are more effective in teaching science and mathematical subjects. On the other hand, professional training was found to have better impact on teacher effectiveness, but when experience factor as a covariate was eliminated, professional training effect was not found significant. Hence, the study concluded that professional training in interaction with experience of teaching improves the quality of teacher effectiveness. Handayani (1985) conducted a study to investigate the relationship between teacher motivation and teacher effectiveness on a sample of 100 teachers. The findings revealed that the self-actualization level of the teacher significantly determines the motivation of the teacher and consequently his / her teacher effectiveness. In his study, Handayani defined self-actualization of teachers as having realistic orientation, possessing spontaneity, being autonomous and independent, having great deal of creativeness, and accepting themselves and other people. He concluded from his study that teachers who possess the high level of these self-actualized characteristics demonstrate strong intrinsic motivation for teaching and tended to be more effective teachers. Some of these characteristics are also used in the present study to assess the teacher effectiveness of women primary teachers in Odisha.

Blalock (1985) attempted to study differences in students' locus of control and self-concept under conditions of more effective and less effective teachers. The results indicated that at the year's end, students become more internal and have a better positive self-concept who studied under more effective teachers than those who studied under less effective teachers. Blalock (1985) conducted a study on a sample 150 school teachers to determine the relationship between their scores in a teaching strategy course and their actual effectiveness during the practicum experience. The findings indicated that how well a teacher scores in a teaching strategy course is not related to his/ her effective teaching. Blalock explained his findings that teacher effectiveness is not only a strategic and planful behavior of the teacher; rather it involves lot of spontaneity available in the personality of the teacher.

Cosper (1986) studied to identify the relationship between planning and teacher effectiveness on a random sample of teachers in public school system throughout the United States. The findings indicated a relationship between teacher effectiveness as rated by principals and teachers planning practices as reported by teachers. It was observed that the teachers who had prior planning to involve more and more students in the proceedings of the class, who explained the concepts with examples from life experiences, and encouraged the students to freely express their point of view were found to be more effective teachers.

Bennett (1986) conducted a study on a sample of 56 teachers and 633 students. The findings indicated that principal-teacher relationship has an impact on teaching effectiveness and this relationship appears to have a complementary dimension. Teachers who were appreciated by the principals as effective teachers were also appreciated by the students. Purser (1986) investigated the relationship between a classification of teacher effectiveness determined by student achievement on a set of teachers' demographic variables on a sample of 87 high school teachers and found that there was no significant relationship between the collective set of demographic teacher variables and teacher effectiveness. Purser concluded that demographic variables such as age, gender, ethnicity, and minority status do not have specific impact on the effectiveness of the teacher.

On the other hand, Kirby and Teddlie (1989) conducted a study to operationalize the concept of reflective practice in teaching and to empirically test the relationship between reflective practice and teacher effectiveness. She found that measures of teacher effectiveness gathered through one hour classroom observation of 102 teachers were significantly correlated with scores on the Reflected Teaching Instrument. Noerrlinger (1987) carried out a study to examine student feedback on teacher effectiveness and those factors, which might influence student feedback on a sample of 19 principals, 76 teachers and 1500 student of elementary classes. Result indicated that elementary students can be reliable source of information on teacher effectiveness. The students agreed with the principals and rated the more effective teachers significantly higher than the less effective teachers on personal interest, classroom management, presentation, guided practice and independent interactions. Significant relationships were also found between students' feedback on teachers' effectiveness and the teacher's age, sex, experience level, ethnic origin and educational level.

Baughn (1987) attempted to identify the standards established by district administration for evaluation of teachers and to determine whether the districts standards reflect the teacher effectiveness. The findings indicated that some of these standards such as experience, education, and training of the teachers are positively associated with the extent of teacher effectiveness. Egins (1987) conducted the study to investigate teacher's perceptions of the impact of some demographic variables on teacher effectiveness and classroom performance of 250 teachers. The findings revealed that years of experiences in teaching, age and gender have significant impact on instructional effectiveness of participating teachers. Duschner (1987) revealed that significant correlations were found between classroom teaching behavior and overall teacher effectiveness. Further most, relationship between classroom behaviors and overall effectiveness varied substantially in magnitude and direction depending on a grade level, academic level and subject area of the teachers.

More (1988) correlated Cattle's 16 personality factors with teacher effectiveness concluded that out of the 16 factors, only six were found to be positively correlated with teacher effectiveness. Those factors are warmth, reasoning, emotional stability, sensitivity, liveliness, and self-reliance. Prakasham (1988) attempted to compare the strength of teacher effectiveness in various types of school organizational climate. The sample comprised of 800 teachers along with 92 principals from 120 government local body, private non-Christian and Christian schools. The findings indicated that teacher of urban schools significantly excelled over teachers employed either in semi-urban schools or school located in industrial areas on both teaching competency and teacher effectiveness and also there existed a significant relationship between teaching competency and teacher effectiveness.

Mincucci (1988) examined whether background characteristics of the teachers prior to employment have any relationship with teacher effectiveness. The results revealed that few background characteristics of teacher viz. educational levels, childhood socio-economic level, mother's education, father's education, and family of teachers, show significant relationships with teacher effectiveness.

Gupta (1988) attempted to study the relationship between age and experience of the teachers and their teacher effectiveness. He used a sample of 46 science teachers and 298 arts teachers from 39 intermediate colleges of Aligarh district and concluded that teacher effectiveness was found to be related to the experience of the teachers. They were found most effective in the 11-15 years-experience group and after that it began to decline. He also found that teacher effectiveness was related to the age of teachers. Teachers were found most effective in the age group of 30-39 years; after that their effectiveness went on diminishing afterwards. Saruis (1989) compared the attitude of 150 elementary school teachers and 25 principals towards the importance of teacher effectiveness characteristics in evaluating teachers. The findings revealed that there was a strong agreement between teachers and principals with respect to which teacher effectiveness characteristics are important for use in conducting teacher evaluation.

Daly (1990) attempted to analyze students' perceptions of teacher effectiveness on 864 students in 54 classes taught by 27 teachers and found that students' perception is a highly reliable source for assessing teacher effectiveness. Deshpande (1993) determined the effectiveness of teachers through the modified version of Popham's performance test on a sample of 27 randomly selected science teachers, 638 students in class IX. The findings indicated that teacher effectiveness as evaluated by the performance test in terms of student achievement was not related to other types of assessment like students' rating, heads' ratings or teacher behavior indices. Singh (1991) conducted a study on the relationship of teaching effectiveness and creativity and intelligence and the composite effect of creativity and intelligence on teaching effectiveness in male and female secondary teachers. The sample included 150 male and 150 female secondary school teachers of Punjab. The findings indicated that among the male and female teachers, teaching effectiveness was positively related with fluency, flexibility, originality, the composite creativity and intelligence.

Edwin (1991) conducted a study to determine the relationship between teacher effectiveness and stage of the teachers' career on 100 elementary school teachers. The findings revealed that performance of a teacher as effective increased at a steady rate until mid- career and then performance drops during late phase of career. Johnson (1992) attempted to examine the perceptions of 434 secondary school teachers from across the United States as what they consider the notion of teacher effectiveness. The findings revealed that communication related skills were rated as of greatest importance by the teachers for teacher effectiveness. Ballard (1992) conducted a study to investigate the perceived effectiveness of teaching and non-teaching principals in the seventh day Adventist secondary educational system. The sample comprised of 840 teachers and 66 principals. The findings revealed that both principals and teachers perceived teaching and non-teaching principals to be equally effective in organizational development, organizational environment and educational program development with regard to years of experience of the teacher or principal, the number of years the teacher had worked for the current principal or the highest academic degree completed by the teacher or principal.

Brodney (1993) attempted to study the relationship between student achievement, student attitude and student perception of teacher effectiveness and the use of journals as a learning tool in mathematics on a sample of 542 students. The findings revealed that students perceive that they have a greater opportunity to learn and perceive that their teachers are more effective when journal writing is used as a tool for learning mathematics.

Singh (1987) conducted a study to examine teacher's effectiveness in relation to gender, area and adjustment to school on a sample of 330 teachers (of both sexes) from 22 higher secondary schools (belonging to rural and urban areas), and concluded that there was a significant difference between male and female teachers in adjustment to school system in favor of male teachers. The co-efficient of correlation between teacher effectiveness scores and adjustment was significant for urban teachers and not significant for rural teachers. Delso (1993) conducted a study on veteran teachers using qualitative interview methods to ascertain what veteran teachers believe effective teacher do. The findings revealed that veteran teachers focused more on increasing students' core academic skills as teacher effectiveness. They also placed little importance on standardized testing as the real academic achievement of students, rather they emphasized on the development of deep processing skills among the students as the true academic progress. These teachers also look to their students to evaluate them to help them get feedback for their teaching and improve their teaching skills. These beliefs of the veteran teachers seemed to align more closely with the teaching culture and teacher thought processes which correlates highly with teacher effectiveness.

Anyalewechi (1994) attempted to identify characteristic traits of effective teachers and factors that teachers consider influential in teacher effectiveness on a sample of 70 secondary school teachers. The findings revealed that there was an agreement on 7 characteristics or traits of effective teachers or factors influencing in teacher effectiveness. These characteristics / factors are student-teacher interaction, effective communication, motivational strategy, personality attributes, evaluation and feedback, subject mastery, and classroom management.

Biswas, Chandra and Tinku (1995) examined the effectiveness of secondary teachers in relation to sex of teacher, location of school (rural and urban), management (Government and Private), type (boys, girls and co-education) and organizational climate of schools. Results reveal that female teachers were more effective; whereas location and management of schools have no significant influence on teacher effectiveness; the teachers of schools with an open climate were most effective while those in schools with a closed climate were least effective. Rao (1995) studied relationship between teacher effectiveness, creativity and inter-personal relationship of teachers. The findings revealed that no significant relation was found between teacher effectiveness and the years of service of the teachers. However, significant relationship was found between teacher effectiveness, creativity and inter-personal relationships of teachers and significant differences existed between rural and urban teachers with reference to inter-personal relationships.

Gupta (1995) examined the relationship between job satisfaction and teacher effectiveness of secondary school teachers and their teaching effectiveness on a sample of 560 teachers of Uttar Pradesh and found that the coefficients of correlation between overall dimensions of job satisfaction of teacher viz. salary and other benefits; community aspect supervision; family life; policies and practices; growth and practices were significantly related with teacher effectiveness.

Wilson (1996) attempted a study focusing on students' and teachers' perceptions of teacher effectiveness on a sample of 41 full-time faculty and 560 students at a community college. The results revealed significant differences is perception between students, between students and teachers and between types of course, on seven categories of teacher effectiveness namely student-teacher interaction, effective communication, motivational strategy, personality attributes, evaluation and feedback, subject mastery, and classroom management.

Indira (1997) tried to find the relationship among teacher effectiveness, work orientation and stress of college teachers on a sample of 220 lecturers working in degree and junior colleges situated in Vizianegaram district and found that the general level of teacher effectiveness prevailing among college teachers was far greater than the mid-point of the scale. Meadows (1997) explored the relationship between teacher leadership style and teacher effectiveness on a sample of 134 instructors and 2,141 students. The findings, through a post hoc analysis, revealed a significant relationship between instructor effectiveness and instructor leadership. Socio-independent instructors received the highest student grades and students' views as enthusiastic mentors. Sikora (1997) conducted a study to examine relationship between personality types and teacher effectiveness of secondary school science teachers. The findings indicated that the teacher's personality may play a significant although limited role in teacher effectiveness.

Bakke (1999) conducted a survey with teachers is the Blue Valley school district in which they were asked to indicate which of a pair of two traits they considered most critical to teacher effectiveness in the classroom. The traits were grouped into clusters which were identified as Interpersonal, Intrapersonal and extra personal. All these clusters were found to have significant contributions to teacher effectiveness having interpersonal traits as the most significant contributor. Other variables considered in the study were gender and number of years of teaching experience. Both these variables were found to have significant impact on teacher effectiveness with the female teachers being found more effective than their male counterparts and more experienced teachers were found to be more effective than less experienced teachers.

Kumar, (1999) studied teacher effectiveness among scheduled caste and non-scheduled caste teachers in relation to their teaching aptitude and self-concept. Sample comprising 502 school teachers (206 SC and 296 NSC teachers) was drawn from government high schools and senior secondary school of 8 districts of Punjab by employing multi-staged stratified random sampling. A three way ANOVA design (2 x 3 x 3) was used to study the main effects and interaction effects of caste, teaching aptitude and self-awareness upon teacher effectiveness of secondary school teachers. Main findings were: (i) caste has no significant effect upon teacher effectiveness irrespective of teaching aptitude and ideal self-concept. (ii) Significant difference exists in teacher effectiveness for teachers belonging to different levels of teaching aptitude (iii) Teachers having high teaching aptitude and ideal self-concept are most effective and (iv) There is no significant interaction among the variables of caste, teaching aptitude and self-concept on teacher effectiveness.

Pandey and Maikhuri(1999) in their study attempted to explore the attitude of effective and ineffective teachers towards teaching profession. The major findings included; (i) There was no significant difference between effective teachers having high or low experience in terms of their profession. (ii) High experienced teachers' attitude was positive towards teaching profession compared to low experienced teachers (iii) Age of effective teacher was not a differentiating factor in their attitude towards teaching profession and (iv) Young ineffective teachers had a negative attitude towards teaching compared to ineffective old teachers.

Allington and Johnson (2002) observed and interviewed 430 fourth grade teachers in the United States who had been identified as excellent teachers. These excellent teachers were found to have used a variety of materials at different levels of teaching, including relevant and meaningful resources beyond text books. Results also revealed that nature of classroom talk of those excellent teachers was highly personal. These teachers were found to encourage productive responses and behaviors among the students, supported the students even if their responses were partially correct, and turn the attention of the students to the processes of learning by encouraging their thinking and reflection.

Khalaf (2000) attempted to explore variables related to chemistry achievement of 12th grade science students in the United Arab Emirates (UAE). The sample included 204 males and 252 females in 66 classes in 60 schools from 10 districts or bureaus of education in the UAE. The results of the multiple linear regression indicated that the factors of prior Student Achievement, Student Perception of Teacher Effectiveness and Teacher Experience and Expertise accounted for 45% of the variance in school chemistry achievement. The results indicated that the strongest predictor of chemistry achievement isstudents'perception of teacher effectiveness or teacher expertise.

Raj (2000) conducted a study on teacher effectiveness of secondary school teachers in relation to motivation to work and job satisfaction. The study was conducted on 100 secondary school teachers from 22 schools (both rural and urban) of Shimla District of Himachal Pradesh. The findings of the study showed that teacher motivation to work has significant effect upon teacher effectiveness, i.e. those having higher level of motivation to work do more effective teaching compared to those who have low motivation for teaching. The conclusions drawn from the study were that teacher effectiveness was positively correlated with the level of motivation to work and teacher effectiveness was not significantly related to job satisfaction.

Quandahl (2001) conducted a study to differentiate the instructional practices of teachers who were more effective, effective and less effective in producing high student achievement. The sample consisted of nine teachers and 208 ethnically diverse students from four schools. The findings suggested that it was possible to discern some common characteristics of teachers who are more effective, effective or less effective. Teachers who were identified as highly effective generally have a strong and positive developmental philosophy which they use in their practice.

Ablert (2002) examined the possible relationship of teacher organizational commitment and teacher effectiveness. The sample comprised of 300 public school teachers who taught in high schools in Illinois. Data analysis indicated that teachers' organizational commitment relating to a positive sense of belonging and a commitment to collaboration resulted in high teacher efficacy and effectiveness. Results suggested that administrators and policy makers should nurture and retain teachers who are committed to the school by fostering a friendly climate and a collaborative environment so that they come out as effective teachers.

Allison and Hirt (2002) conducted a study to compare the teaching effectiveness of part time and full time clinical nursing teachers. The sample included two groups: clinical nursing students in Associate Degree Nursing programs at schools in a mid-Atlantic state and the part time and full time faculty who taught those students. Results of the study indicated that students rank part time faculty as significantly less effective than full time faculty on each of the five categories of teacher effectiveness measures such as Teaching ability, Nursing competence, Evaluation, Interpersonal relationship and Personality traits. The findings also revealed that there is no significant difference in the students' rating of teacher effectiveness and the self-ratings of the teachers themselves.

Kagathala (2002) studied teacher effectiveness of teachers of secondary schools in Gujarat in relation to area of their schools, sex, educational qualifications, experience of teaching, type of school, teacher's personality and caste. Teacher effectiveness scale (Developed by the investigator), and creative personality inventory were administered upon 1800 teachers (1290 male and 510 female) of secondary schools of different parts of Gujarat. Result of the study showed that teacher effectiveness of secondary schools in

Gujarat was found to be of average; The teachers of urban area are superior than rural area in teacher effectiveness; Sex of the teacher does not affect the teacher effectiveness; The teachers with master's degree possess more teacher effectiveness than bachelor degrees holders; The effect of experience of teaching on the teacher effectiveness is found increasing up to the experience of 19 years but it is found to be decreasing after that level of experience; The teachers of boys schools are found to be more effective than girls and coeducational schools; The teacher having high creative personality are found superior to the teacher having low creative personality with respect to teacher effectiveness; No effect of caste of teacher on the teacher effectiveness was found.

Singh (2002) conducted a comparative study of job satisfaction of teacher educators in relation to their values, attitude towards teaching and teacher effectiveness. Results, of the study showed that job satisfaction is positively correlated with social value, hedonistic value, power value. Attitude towards teaching and teacher effectiveness is positively correlated with job satisfaction.

Castle (2003) attempted a study to develop a transformative critical pedagogy that teachers are currently required to teach. The multisensory component of the pedagogy was designed to assist teachers in developing effective learning and teaching strategies. The findings revealed that a rigorous academic program combined with a critical socially constructed teaching/learning environment based on interaction, discovery and problem solving contributed to strong teacher effectiveness and students' learning was very effective.

Selsor (2003) sought to examine the differential importance in the primary dimensions of effective teaching as perceived by a sample of rural and suburban college students. Students from 4 community colleges (N=337) were asked to rate 31 descriptive statements which encompasses 9 dimensions of effective teaching and respond to one open ended question as stated on the student's evaluation of educational quality. The results indicated that college students gave highest rating for teacher effectiveness to dimensions related to the communication skills of the teachers, followed by teacher's enthusiasm, individual rapport and group interaction.

Punia (2004) attempted to examine intuitive abilities and human resources of effective teachers. The findings indicated that effective teachers are well aware of the need to find problems and setting the objectives of their teaching. It is observed that in the entire process of goal setting for teaching in the class, the intuitive abilities of the teachers have a great role to play. Vijaylakshmi and Mythill (2004) studied the influence of personal variables (age, marital status, and gender) and professional variables (experience, qualification, subject of teaching, designation, level of college type of college management) on the teacher effectiveness and work orientation of 220 teachers working in junior colleges, degree colleges, and professional colleges of Viziangaram district of Andhra Pradesh. Results showed that there was significant difference in teacher effectiveness between the teachers up to 35 years of age and beyond that age difference was not found. In fact, no differences were observed in teacher effectiveness between married and unmarried teachers, among teachers with different designation and also teachers working in junior and degree colleges. However, regarding their work orientation, significant difference existed between married and unmarried teachers, male and female teachers, teachers of different cadres, between junior and degree college staff and government and private college teachers. On the other hand, they also reported a moderate positive relationship between teacher effectiveness and their work orientation. It was concluded in the study that teachers of above 35 years age, married teachers, female teachers, assistant professors and degree college teacher are more effective than their counterparts.

Amandeep and Gurpreet (2005) concluded that female teachers are more effective in their teaching than male teachers in primary and higher secondary classes although male and female teachers do not differ significantly in their teaching competency. They concluded that although teaching competency is a crucial factor for teacher effectiveness, other important psychosocial factors also play significant roles in the effectiveness of a teacher.

Pandit and Surwade (2006) in their study on effect of emotional maturity on teacher effectiveness found that female teachers were emotionally more matured and stable than male teachers, and more emotionally matured teachers were more effective. Cheung (2006) found that female teachers were significantly more efficacious than male teachers particularly in teaching primary school students. He also observed that years of teaching experience were weakly but significantly related to levels of efficacy, but educational level of the teacher did not have a significant effect on his / her teaching effectiveness.

Haaris and Rutledge (2007) compared research on the theoretical models and predictors of teacher effectiveness with those of other occupations, focusing on three specific predictors of worker effectiveness: cognitive ability, personality, and education. The comparison of the teachers and other workers yields a variety of ways in which research on teacher effectiveness might be improved and expanded. First, the worker literature illustrates specific theoretical models, such as job-organization-fit, that complement existing models regarding the work of teachers. The potential value of extending worker models to teaching in this way is reinforced by the fact that the three teacher characteristics mentioned above predict effectiveness in similar ways among teachers and other workers. Second, by outlining multiple models of effectiveness, it is possible to identify the important dimensions on which they vary, such as the unit of analysis and the assumed roles of the teacher in relation to the organization. Third, research on other workers highlights some ways to improve the measurement of the three predictors and teacher effectiveness, going beyond the use of test scores.

Newa (2007) studied teacher effectiveness in relation to work satisfaction, media utilization and attitude towards the use of information and communication technology among secondary school teachers of Nepal. The sample of the study consisted of 300 government and private school teachers of Kathmandu valley. Results of the study show that : For the total sample of government and private schools, teacher effectiveness was found to be positively related with job satisfaction, media utilization and attitude towards information and technology; No significant interaction was found between school type and teachers of academic stream with regard to teacher effectiveness; More effective teachers exhibited better work satisfaction, attitude towards media utilization and attitude towards information and technology; More effective teachers and less effective teachers of science, math, language, social sciences of secondary school exhibited significant differences in job satisfaction, media utilization and attitude towards information and technology.

Kaur (2008) studied job satisfaction, occupational, stress and value dimensions as correlates of teacher effectiveness. A sample of 1000 teachers was selected from Government secondary schools of four districts of Punjab, namely; Ludhiana, Patiala, Mukatsar and Moga. Data was collected by different scales like teacher effectiveness scale by Kumar and Mutha, Job satisfaction scale by Sharma and Singh, study of value scale by Ojhaand self-constructed occupational stress scale. The result of the study pointed out that: The government secondary school teachers are average in their effectiveness; highly effective teachers were more satisfied with their jobs than less effective teaches. Further the study has shown that job satisfaction is a positive correlate of teacher effectiveness; Occupational stress is a negative correlate of teacher effectiveness. Also the teachers who are under high occupational stress are less effective. Moreover, theoretical, aesthetic and social values are found to be positive correlated, whereas, economic and political values are found to be negative correlates of teacher effectiveness.

Rockoff et al. (2010), in their in-depth survey on new Math teachers in New York City, collected information on a number of predictors of teacher effectiveness including content knowledge, cognitive ability, personality traits, feeling of self-efficacy, and scores on a commercially available teacher selection instrument. They found that individually only a few of these predictors had statistically significant relationship with student and teacher outcomes. However, when all of these variables were combined into primary factors summarizing cognitive and non-cognitive teacher skills, they found that both factors had a modest and significant relationship with student and teacher outcomes, particularly with student test scores. These results suggest that while there may not be a single factor that can predict success in teacher effectiveness, using a broad set of measures can help schools improve the quality of their teachers.

Schulte et al. (2008) analyzed the characteristics of effective high school teachers as perceived by 615 college students in relation to gender, ethnicity, student's status and generational status. Qualitative analyses revealed the presence of 24 themes in teacher effectiveness such as caring, communication, creative, disciplinarian, fairness, flexible, friendly, fun, knowledgeable, listening, manages classroom, uses different modalities, involving, motivating, organized, passion for teaching, patience, builds relationships, shows respect to others, challenges, service, teaches well and good personality.

Sridhar and Badiei (2008) compared the teacher efficacy in India and Iran. Statistically no significant difference in general teaching efficacy scores were found between two countries. A statistical difference was found between male teachers in the two countries in terms of personal teaching efficacy. Iranian male teachers had high personal efficacy than their Indian counterparts. However, female teachers in the two countries did not show statistical difference in teacher efficacy. Also, no significant difference was found in teacher efficacy for number of years of teaching experience.

Verma (2010) while discussing inclusive education lacks stress on teacher development, by building competencies of all 'regular teacher' to deal with diverse population of students and to learn pedagogical strategies that facilitate the learning of all students in their classroom. These include certain specific competencies i.e. foundational, practical and reflective competencies.

Diwan (2010) too, lays stress on increasing teaching efficacy in order to strengthen under-resourced schools to serve the cause of educability of young learners in the disadvantaged groups of society such as urban slums, SCs/STs and in remote forest and hilly areas. It is a gigantic task that can be accomplished with the support of competent teachers showing a feeling of empathy and compassion along with being knowledgeable and with good communication skills. In a similar vein, Hameed and Manjustha (2010) tried to explain teacher efficacy as a correlate of teaching styles and organizational culture and it was reported that school culture has a significant bearing on teacher efficacy.

The above extensive review and the chronological account of research on teacher effectiveness pointed to a large number of variables influencing effectiveness of the teachers which includes institutional variables (quality and quantity of teachers, remuneration of teachers, working conditions of the teachers, facilities such as instructional materials, and well-equipped laboratories and libraries), socio-cultural variables (socio-cultural background of the students, level and type of education of parents and siblings, interpersonal relationship among family members), and system variables (type of management, school climate, feedback provisions etc.). However, most of the studies have emphasized on teacher variables as the strongest predictor of teacher effectiveness. Particularly, the psychosocial attributes and personality characteristics of the teachers are found to have striking impact on teacher effectiveness. Several of the teacher variables like gender, age, teaching experience, and personality characteristics have been reported as profound factors of teacher effectiveness. Numerous Indian studies cited above have also reported on the efficacy of the teacher variables in developing effective teachers. In the line of those researches, the present study is planned to examine the effectiveness of women primary teachers in Odisha with respect to their psychosocial attributes and psychological capital. The following are reasons as to why the researcher was fascinated about women primary teachers in Odisha.

Significance of Women Teachers

Moreover, to achieve the goals of Education For All (EFA) and the Millennium Development Goals, researchers have emphasized that attention should be focused on the provision of quality teachers for primary and secondary school education who will be able to teach and equip the students with the opportunities they need to optimize their potentials and contribute to the growth and development of the society and humanity. Presently, the delivery of basic education all across the world including India is more or less in the hands of the female teachers, as statistics from the Federal Ministry of Education (2013) have shown that the percentage of female teachers, especially at the elementary level, is higher than that of the male teachers (female teachers- 73.3%, male teachers- 27.7%). Female teachers have been found to be warm, patient, and meticulous. They have also been found to be affected more emotionally and psychosocially than males by situations, events, gender roles and role conflicts, and socio-cultural demands, while also experiencing more professional burnout (Singh, 2016). Therefore, investigating some of the factors affecting female teachers' effectiveness will go a long way in improving the quality of the majority of teachers who will deliver the nation's educational goals. Such investigation could provide valuable information for a better understanding of the female teachers and make way for development of necessary interventions that could help them perform their professional duties at their best. This will invariably contribute to improving the condition of the educational system in India. Hence, the present research was proposed to investigate the psychosocial attributes and psychological capital of women primary teachers in Odisha.

Studies on Women Teachers

Studies (Babu& Fathima, 2017) conducted on female teachers reported that female teachers are a special group of people, who although in the majority, were often not given adequate attention and consideration. In addition, most of them were inclined to lose their enthusiasm for work, had little interest in personal accomplishment, took no pride in their profession, and had a lower efficiency in the work (Liu, 2005).Several studies have been conducted on female teachers which have reported that there is gender discrimination against the women teachers in many parts of the world. Mallam (2005) in his study of the impact of gender of teacher on students' attitudes toward mathematics found that female students learned mathematics better when they were taught by female teachers. Akiri & Ugborugbo (2009) in their studies of job satisfaction among Nigerian teachers, revealed that female teachers found their jobs more satisfying than male teachers did. Sargent &Hannum (2003) found that gender does not have a statistically significant relationship with teachers' job satisfaction, though female teachers appeared to be more satisfied with their teaching career. In a study conducted by Ijaiya (2008) on the belief system of 60 principals and vice principals on the productivity of teachers in their schools, it was reported that the majority of them considered experience, qualifications, and marital status are major factors of productivity among teachers. Male principals, however, held the view that male teachers were more productive than the females, whom they considered disadvantaged by domestic responsibilities. Researchers agreed that variations in life situations, events, and gender roles affect female teachers in the society; the extent to which these may affect their effectiveness as teachers have also been reported in several studies.

The above discussions about women teachers definitely point to their significant role in the socio-educational processes of the society and also to the extent they take the responsibility in the process of social development. No doubt, the women teachers anywhere in the world constitute a special group who needs to be understood, explained, and supported. Odisha, being a backward state in the Indian republic and having its primary education largely in the hands of women teachers, is definitely in a need to know the psychosocial aspects of the women teachers and thereby carry out appropriate intervention programs to help them improve their teacher effectiveness skills.

Psychosocial Attributes of Teachers

The idea of psychosocial attributes of the teachers for the present study was based on the contribution of Chatopadhyay (2014) who developed a battery of test to assess the socio-emotional competence of teachers in the Indian context which she designated as Psychosocial Attribute Measurement Battery (PAMB). The battery consisted of 10 different measures to assess the psychosocial attributes of the teachers. The following are the elaboration of the constructs of Chatopadhyay's psychosocial attributes of teachers citing evidences from research literature.

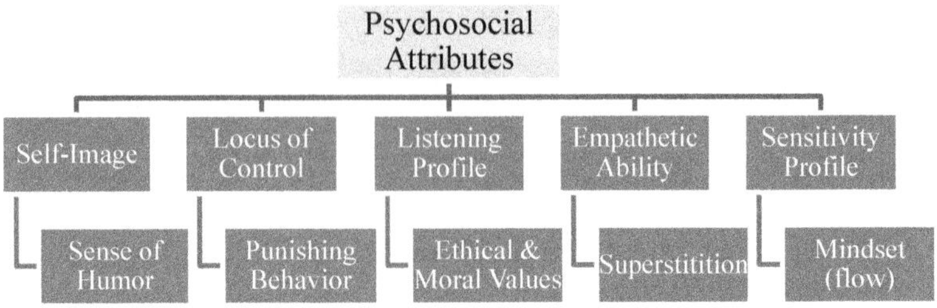

Self-image and teacher effectiveness. Gold and Roth (1993) defined self-image as "a process of getting in touch with your feelings and behaviors". They observed that increased self-image of teachers involves a more accurate understanding of how students affect their emotional processes and behaviors and in turn, how they affect the students as well. Self-image is more important for teachers when they work with students having emotional or behavioral problems. Richardson (2001) pointed out that these students often help teachers to reflect on the best in them and help them to be more effective teachers. He observed in his study that the development of teachers largely depends on their willingness to ask themselves as to which of their behaviors are helping or hindering their personal and professional growth. Underhill (1991) reported that teachers who undertake to learn from their experiences in the classroom became more effective teachers. Richardson & Shupe (2003) in their study on emotionally disturbed students identified five strategies to help the teachers to increase self-image and also reported on their improved teacher effectiveness by using the following strategies.

(i) Diffuse emotional triggers- The first strategy involves whether the teacher is taking proactive steps to identify and defuse his own emotional triggers. Cheney and Barringer (1995) asserted that students with emotional and behavioral problems affect the teachers on a very personal level. Unfortunately, teacher education does not highlight the connection between a teacher's self-image and his or her ability to build and maintain meaningful emotional relationships with students. They observed in their study that teachers need to learn how to recognize signs of emotional problems among the students. Fritz (2004), a pioneer in working with students with emotional disturbances, emphasized that self-image is a key ingredient for appropriately dealing with these students. He said that as teachers, we have a room, equipment, materials, a curriculum, instructional methods, and grades, but beyond all these, we have ourselves. What happens to us emotionally in the process of teaching is the critical factor in determining our effectiveness. Helping students only begins with understanding ourselves, particularly our own emotional processes that occur in the midst of conflict. Although psychological soundness and effective interpersonal skills are essential characteristics for teachers (Kaufman, 1997; Webber, Anderson, & Otey, 1991), certain students can provoke even the most concerned, reasonable, and dedicated teachers to act in impulsive, and rejecting ways (Long, 1996a).

Students experiencing stress are likely to affect us personally. But, few of us possess the inner peace to respond to the situation in a calm and professional manner. Fritz suggested that awareness of our primary emotional triggers improves our chances of making rational decisions based on conscious choice, thereby helping us to be effective teachers. Further, Long (1996a) asserted that negative feelings such as anger, frustration, and disdain among the teachers are more likely to generate a counterproductive power struggle between the teacher and the students. However, teachers who are aware of their own emotional processes are more likely to minimize the frequency and intensity of these counterproductive power struggles.

(ii) *Using positive reinforcement*- The second strategy involves whether the teacher is paying attention to what he needs to pay attention to. Most teachers recognize the power and necessity of using positive reinforcement (e.g., Johns & Carr, 1995) as effective teaching strategies. By consciously noticing and reinforcing positive behavior, the classroom becomes a more positive environment, one in which the recognition of both academic and behavioral accomplishments leads to increased student self-esteem (Fagan, 1996). In an extensive study of effective teaching behaviors, Larrivee (2004) found that "giving positive feedback" in the classroom is strongly correlated with students' performance. Johns et al., (2005) in their study on primary school students reported that teachers who give at least 70% positive comments in the classroom are considered to be effective teachers.

Researchers have also found that teachers' praise is positively linked not only to improved behavioral and academic outcomes of students but also to their emotional development (Sutherland & Wehby, 2001a).

(iii) Enhance self-awareness- The third strategy to enhance the teacher's self-awareness is whether the teacher is using effective strategies to reduce burnout and nurture his own mental health. Teaching students and appropriately dealing with their emotions is one of the most challenging tasks (Cheney & Barringer, 1995). Sometimes teachers are faced with enormous pressures and challenges and report high levels of emotional exhaustion. They are primarily evaluated on their ability to help students make tangible, academic improvements (Long, 1996a, Male & May, 1997); yet they are also expected to assume multiple roles, such as model, disciplinarian, surrogate parent, social worker, and counselor. Many teachers find it difficult to perform all these roles in the midst of increasing class sizes. Teachers find themselves struggling to find time to adequately cover each of the learning objectives while also attending to the emotional needs of their students. Teacher stress can adversely affect the teachers, their students, and the classroom climate. Cheney and Barringer (1995) found that stress among the teachers can be manifested as (a) a reluctance to consider factors beyond the immediately observable behavior of the student, and (b) a rigid focus on school rules as a way of coping with problematic situations. To survive and thrive in the classroom, teachers must develop effective strategies for

regularly monitoring and managing their own stress. Teachers need safe places to express their feelings and frustrations and recharge their positive emotions. In a survey of special education teachers, Pullis (1992) found that talking with supportive colleagues is one of the most effective coping strategies. In fact, 96% of teachers rated collaborating and talking with colleagues as one of their most effective strategies for coping with school stress. However, teachers need to recognize the difference between the need to vent and a pattern of negativity and complaining. Venting is only helping the teacher to release the pent-up feelings. If this process only adds to their stress and frustration, they might employ a different strategy. Teachers must regularly assess their coping skills and seek out positive colleagues and role models who will engage them in supportive, constructive dialogue and thereby encouraging their positive self-esteem.

(iv) Using sense of humor- The fourth strategy to enhance the teacher's self-image is helping the teacher to use an appropriate sense of humor to build relationships, diffuse conflict, engage learners, and manage his own stress. A number of educators have pointed out that an appropriate sense of humor is absolutely essential for teacher effectiveness (Richardson, 2006; Webber et al., 1991). Some students are often victims of a variety of emotional stressors (e.g., poor reading skills, changing family structure, parental abuse and neglect) and are likely to direct their hurt and frustration at teachers and peers. Those students need to be held accountable for their behavior. However, if

teachers take their actions personally or too seriously, they place them at risk for both overreacting and burnout. For example, while working as a high school counselor, Shupe (2012) was informed that 80% of the disciplinary referrals to the principal came from only 10% of the teachers. When asked if there were commonalities among those teachers, the principal remarked, they all seem to take themselves and their jobs too seriously. They seem unhappy when they teach. Ironically, while they have very little tolerance for 'acting-out' behaviors, students tend to act out more in their classes. On the other hand, "teachers with a sense of humor are usually happy, relaxed, fun-loving, and reinforcing to others (Webber et al., 1991). A recent study supported these observations. Talbot and Lumden (2013) found that teachers who were more likely to use humor in their classroom reported lower emotional exhaustion and a higher sense of personal accomplishment. Also, many studies have pointed out that an appropriate sense of humor is an effective strategy for engaging students who seem to be disengaged (Johns & Carr, 1995; Webber et al., 1991). These authors also noted that humor is also one of the most effective means of de-escalating potential crisis situations in classrooms. Webber et al. observed that it is difficult for a student to continue to act aggressively or destructively while he or she is laughing.

Crowley (1993) interviewed students regarding helpful teacher attitudes and behaviors and found that students repeatedly talked about the relevance of humor in the classroom. Victor Borge, the comedian, when said, "Laughter is the shortest distance between two people" in fact wanted to pass on the message to an audience of teachers. Sultanoff (1999) asserted that one of the greatest potential gifts we can provide for children is to present ourselves as "humor beings." By living in a humorous perspective, teachers can teach children to effectively manage life's challenges with far less stress. Having a sense of humor in the classroom is less about telling jokes and more about maintaining a relaxed and upbeat attitude. Teachers who have an appropriate sense of humor convey to their students that they enjoy their jobs, like their students, relish playful exchanges, and do not take themselves too seriously. Most importantly, they recognize the difference between humor that hurts and humor that heals. Richardson (2001) noted that humor that hurts is sarcastic, caustic, and pushes people away from one another, whereas humor that heals is sensitive, good natured, defuses difficult situations, and brings people closer together. As teachers, we need to periodically assess our use of humor in the classroom and make adjustments when warranted.

(v) Acknowledgement- The fifth strategy for self-awareness of a teacher involves regularly acknowledging that he is significantly making a difference in the lives of students. In conducting workshops for professionals who work with youth with emotional and behavioral disabilities, Shupe (2012) shared the following story of a young boy rescuing starfish on the beach: A young boy was walking along the beach in the middle of a summer day. As the tide

was retreating, he noticed thousands of starfish washed up on the dry sand. As the boy began throwing starfish back into the ocean, a man was passing by and said, "Son, look how many are there, you will never make a difference." Smiling, the boy looked at the starfish in his hand, threw it into the ocean, and declared, "I'll make a difference to that one." The plight of students with disabilities is analogous to starfish washed up on the dry sand. It is easy to become paralyzed by the magnitude of the task and fail to recognize ways teachers are making a difference. Kaufman and Wong (1991) found that teachers who perceive themselves as having the ability to bring about desired student results are more likely to perceive their students as teachable and worthy of their attention and effort. In fact, one study defined teacher efficacy as "the extent to which the teacher believes he or she has the capacity to affect student performance" (Bergman, McLaughlin, Bass, Pauly, & Zellman, 1977). These teachers with a high sense of self-efficacy were also less likely to personalize the misbehaviors of students and more likely to maintain an attitude of tolerance for difficult students. Recognizing ways that they and others are making a difference can affect the teachers' perceived self-efficacy. Although many teachers make a habit of overextending themselves, burnout is just as likely to result from a persistent feeling that they are not truly making a difference. The Starfish story is one simple way to encourage ourselves and others to be proactive in acknowledging the contributions of teachers.

Many teachers have not received adequate training to recognize how their own psychological histories and personalities affect their interactions with students. Although the success of teacher to reach and teach students depends on many factors, increasing their self-awareness is an important area in which teachers have more direct control. If teachers make conscious, ongoing efforts to increase their self-awareness, they are likely to enhance their effectiveness and their job satisfaction. We must remember that the overall attitude of the teacher and the classroom climate affect students much more than most other techniques or interactions.

Locus of control and teacher effectiveness. Locus of control research was derived from Rotter's (1966) social learning theory which hypothesized that individual differences existed as to perceived responsibility for one's own actions and the individual's sense of personal control of reinforcement. Individuals who perceived their reinforcement as contingent upon their own behavior, attributes or capacities were described by Rotter (1966) as having an internal locus of control. Rotter labeled individuals as external if they did not perceive a relationship between their own behavior and the reinforcement.

Inspired by developed models of teacher expectancy influences, there has been a resurgence of interest in the behaviors and attitudes of effective and successful teachers. Among the attitudinal variables receiving increasing attention are teacher’s perceptions of personal control over or responsibility for learner achievement. Whether or not teachers see themselves as capable or incapable - influences the achievement of learners (Woolfolk, 2007).

Findley & Cooper (1983), in an extensive literature search, reported the link between teacher's locus of control and its impact on the academic attitude, behavior and achievement of the students. They observed that teachers who had confidence in their teaching ability were more internally controlled and they have a strong and continued impact on the academic attitude, behavior, and performance of their students. Similarly, Murray & Staebler (1974) examined the relationship of teachers' locus of control with student achievement on several standardized tests. The results indicated that both male and female students, regardless of their locus of control, gained more on the achievement measures under internal teachers than under external teachers. They have also reported significant associations between teacher's locus of control and teachers' management of the classroom environment. Internal teachers had fewer disciplinary commands given to students, lower rates of inappropriate student behavior, higher rates of student directed activity, and they carried out classroom instruction more efficiently. Other studies also had shown evidence of a relationship between teachers' locus of control and their use of effective classroom management techniques. Brophy (2006) reviewed the findings of the Texas Teacher Effectiveness Study and found that internal teachers assumed better responsibility for classroom events and maintained organized learning environments. This research also found that internal teachers took a more active role in the instructional process.

Several other studies which have examined the relation between locus of control and teacher characteristics (e.g., Rose & Medway, 1993) reported that internal teachers were more likely to implement successful innovative techniques and motivate students. Studies examining teacher variables of age, gender, and race indicated that internality of teachers increased with age and that female teachers appeared to be more internally controlled than males (Richardson, 2006). Richardson observed that young teachers because of their lack of experience may be overly concerned about issues critical to their successful classroom functioning. Since young teachers may be more concerned with classroom management, they may see themselves as being controlled by environmental events and, therefore, adopt more of an external locus of control. Guskey (1981) reported that female teachers consistently assumed greater responsibility for the learning outcomes of their students than male teachers. Smith (1986) hypothesized that teaching tended to be perceived as a female occupation and, therefore, female teachers may be more comfortable in the job and more internally controlled.

Krause, Bochner, Duchesne & McMaugh (2010) reported that compared to teachers with external locus of control, teachers with internal locus of control are found to spend more time on intellectual and academic activities. They are also found to be more active in social activities, and determined against hardships as well as strongly objecting to self-limitations. These teachers perceive themselves as independent and assume responsibility. They are found to exhibit independence in their social actions as well as such other attributes as being consistent and judicious about their profession (O'Donnell, Reeve & Smith, 2009; Krause et al., 2010; Slavin, 2009; Woolfolk, 2007). On the other hand, teachers with external locus of control exhibit traits such as low self-esteem with increased depressive state, feeling of despair, loneliness, conformist and passive, not trusting the self and others, and aggressive (O'Donnel et al., 2009). In yet another study, analysis has shown that teachers scoring high on a measure of internal locus of control are significantly more likely to be perceived as high in overall teaching competence by a set of evaluators in comparison with teachers indicating a lesser degree of internal control orientation (Scheck & Rhodes, 2001).

Several research studies have also been conducted regarding learners locus of control. Woolfolk (2007) reported that Locus of control can be very important in explaining a learner's performance. For example, researchers have found that learners who are high in internal locus of control have better grades and test scores than do learners of the same intelligence who are low in internal locus of control (Pajares& Graham, 1999; Zimmerman, 2000;

Ormrod, 2008). According to Slavin (2009), in other studies it has been found that locus of control is the second most important predictor after ability, of a learner's academic achievement.

The concern for improving academic achievement has increased in recent years. A study conducted by Adeyinka & Adeniyi, (2011) indicated that a significant relationship exists between teachers' locus of control and students' academic achievement. The study also revealed that teachers' self-efficacy and locus of control predicted 49% of the learners' academic achievement. The implications of these findings on stakeholders in educational industry, curriculum planners, educational psychologists and practitioners were suggested (Adeyinka & Adeniyi, 2011). Several other researchers (Adeyemo 2001, 2006; Aremu, 2000; Zimmerman, 2000; Bong and Skaalvik, 2003) have also reported that academic achievement of students is associated with the locus of control of the teachers.

Listening profile and teacher effectiveness. Good listening skills for the teachers are needed to develop empathy and understanding with the students and to assess whether they understand what they are being taught. Listening skills also help in negotiating with students and defusing any potential classroom conflicts. Butler (2012) compared the academic performance of 400 college students under three categories of teachers. The first category was very good and proactively listening teachers (keep composure and patience in listening to students), the second category was also very good but reactively listening teachers (make arguments, blame the students, threaten for punishment) and the third group was teachers with poor listening ability (avoid students and take plea of other works when students want to discuss). Butler observed that college students performed best in almost all subjects under proactively listening teachers; and even they performed significantly better under reactively listening teachers than under teachers with indifference or poor listening ability.

Similarly, Hargreaves (2012) reported from a study including both men and women high school teachers that listening is the most powerful tool of teachers which helped them to learn many things personal about the students. In the study, it was observed that teachers with a good listening profile were able to describe more elaborately any student than teachers with poor listening profile. The important thing was that these teachers were able to elaborately describe the students' curiosity, aptitude, and interest and also what sparks their curiosity. He also reported that teacher's listening has a strong motivating power for both student and the teacher in the class. Teachers who engage part of their classroom time listening to students become more motivated to take classes and students become more willing to attend to their classes than teachers who only teach in the class without listening to the students. From his study of teacher-student interaction analysis, Hudson (2017) reported five reasons why listening is important for teachers. According to him teacher's listening to students make the students feel respected, motivate them for study, and help them to develop self-confidence. It also helps the teacher to find out what is really going on with the students, to provide an effective role model to students, and to get appropriate feedback from parents. Hence, listening profile of the teachers is very powerful tool for effectiveness in teaching.

Empathetic ability and teacher effectiveness. As teachers' empathic abilities increase, it seems likely that they would be better able to understand and respond appropriately to their students (Butler, 2012). According to Butler, empathetic ability is one of the best gifts of teachers which bring the students and the teachers into emotional proximity.

Deiro (1996) who conducted a study on 1700 teachers from different communities concluded that teachers who lack in empathetic ability are perceived by the students with fear and anger while teachers with high empathetic ability are perceived by them with love and affection. He further observed that mentally retarded and hearing impaired children very quickly identified empathetic teachers from their group photographs but they were very late in identifying the non-empathetic teachers.

Garriston and Liston (2004) when made the content analysis of students' thoughts, opinions, and feelings observed that each student has a mental framework that closely resembles an empathetic teacher while very few students' mental framework resembled to non-empathetic teachers. They further reported that teachers cannot expect to have an impact on intellectual development of students without becoming involved in their emotional processes and empathy is the best emotional transaction between the teacher and students.

Sensitivity profile and teacher effectiveness. Every class is a combination of students having varied socio-cultural needs. The teachers' sensitivity profile refers to his /her awareness about these socio-cultural needs of the students and act purposively to address these needs of the students. For example, considering a class in the Odisha set up, students coming from different caste groups, socioeconomic groups and minority groups do not have same socio-cultural needs. Some of them lack in parental support, some of them require financial help, while some others are victims of social taboos. Hence, they require teachers' support for their needs which can be addressed by the teacher's sensitivity to the issues.

Bloom (2008) reported from a study involving students from different socio-cultural backgrounds that socio-culturally sensitive teachers create positive outcomes for all students and demonstrate better classroom management. Every student in the class has a better feeling of security, confidence and willingness to learn. In his paper, "Affirming diversity: The socio-political context of multicultural education", Nieto (2004) reported that multicultural sensitivity among the teachers is the most significant factor contributing to teacher effectiveness. Teachers who are identified as having social prejudice are found to have not only negative impact on students' performance, but they are also negatively evaluated by parents and colleagues. Gorton (2003) has reported that teachers' sensitive profile is negatively associated with bullying behavior among students. He reported that same students before and after the class of a teacher with low sensitive profile become more unruly and found to be engaged in bullying behavior.

Sense of humor and teacher effectiveness. Lovern (2008) carried out a study examining the relationship between teachers' sense of humor and students' behavior and performance. She reported that teachers' sense of humor is positively related to learners' intrinsic motivation and better academic achievements. She also reported that teachers' sense of humor is more effective in the classes of difficult subjects as she observed that sense of humor is most effective in the mathematics classes. Torok et al., (2004) reported that sense of humor is one instructional tool that teachers can use in the classroom to overcome the stressful and boring feelings among the students.

Punishing behavior and teacher effectiveness. Teachers punishing behavior has been a controversial issue in the research literature. While most of research findings suggest that teacher's punishing behavior is ultimately a handicap for the students, some of the research also point to punishment management as a teacher skill to induce discipline among the students. However, a large number of researches claim that punishing behavior of teachers for primary school children has negative impact on students' development. Shah (2012) reviewing on the impact of teachers' behavior on students' self regulation pointed out that there is a strong positive correlation between the teachers' friendly relationship and students' eagerness for discipline. There is a positive and significant relationship between teachers' amount of respect for students and students disciplined behavior. There is also a significant relationship between teachers' self-regulation model and students' acceptance of discipline and he categorically pointed out that punishment is no solution to students' problem. Arigbo and Adeogun (2018) in a paper on effect of punishment on students' academic performance have reported that punishment is negatively related to students' academic performance. They also reported that 79.17% of the students in their study disagree that punishment was administered in school on right cause, and 60% of the students disagree with the statement that teachers give punishment to maintain discipline in the class.

Ethical and moral values and teacher effectiveness. A study of Pantic and Wubbels (2012) examined the impact of teachers' ethical and moral value on their interpersonal relationship with students and arousal of cultural competence among the students. They observed that teachers' moral value has a strong impact on the affiliation and control of the students. They have also reported a positive association between teachers' moral values and students metacognitive and motivational components of cultural competence.

Superstition and teacher effectiveness. Superstitious beliefs are irrational beliefs and notions held by human beings, which are based on fear, magical thinking, ignorance, and blind faith. These beliefs and notions do not have any basis in logic, facts, common sense, or in reality. Some of these beliefs include beliefs in God, ghost, charms, witches, black magic, miracles and black medicines. Olorundare (1998) reported from a study on Nigerian students that superstitious beliefs of teachers have a negative effect on students learning of science and tend to impede students' conceptualization of scientific knowledge by creating an existing prior knowledge which is in contrast with the scientific knowledge to be learned. Albert (2010) in a study of relationship between scientific literacy and African teachers' superstitious beliefs pointed out that science and superstition are not compatible with teachers and superstitious teachers not only are poor science teachers, they do have also less impact on students' performance. Evidence also exist to suggest that African students do not utilize what they learn in science in real life (Shumba, 1999) because they go through the ordeal of memorizing what is necessary to pass in the examination after which they return to the security of their traditional beliefs. The international association for the evaluation of educational achievement (IEA) also pointed to the poor performance of students in science in developing countries when compared to their counterparts in the developed countries which they assigned to their superstitious traditional beliefs (Postlethwaite & Wiley, 2010).

Flow mindset and teacher effectiveness. There is increasing awareness among educators on the importance of fostering a flow mindset among the students and teachers. A recent survey by the Education Week Research Center (2016) indicated that 45 percent of teachers in USA were well acquainted with the concept of flow mindset, and almost all of them believe that nurturing a flow mindset in their students would improve their learning outcomes. Some teachers believe teaching is a natural ability that you either have or don't have (i.e., a fixed mindset) whereas others believe teaching ability is something that can be developed (i.e., a growth mindset). Just as with students, there are benefits of a flow mindset for the teachers. Gero (2013) reported from a study that teachers, who believe they can improve, seek out opportunities to learn, try to gather feedbacks for their teaching and appreciate appropriate constructive criticisms to improve their teaching while those with a fixed mindset are found as hesitant learners and take criticisms as a sign of their limited teaching ability. Auten (2013) reported from a study that teachers with flow mindset are not afraid to try new things in their classrooms and they continue to search out new pedagogical techniques in teaching. They encourage success in their students and help them to perseverate in their study. These teachers are mostly appreciated by the students as effective teachers.

Psychological Capital of the Teachers

Psychological capital is defined as the positive and developmental state of an individual as characterized by high self-efficacy, optimism, hope and resiliency. Hope is defined as a positive motivational state where two basic elements - successful feeling of agency (or goal oriented determination) and pathways (or proactively planning to achieve those goals) interact. Self efficacy is defined as people's confidence in their ability to achieve a specific goal in a specific situation. Optimism is a mental attitude reflecting a belief or hope that the outcome of some specific endeavor or outcomes in general, will be positive, favorable, and desirable. Resilience is defined as a positive way of coping with adversity or distress. It is defined as an ability to recuperate from stress, conflict, failure, change or increase in responsibility.

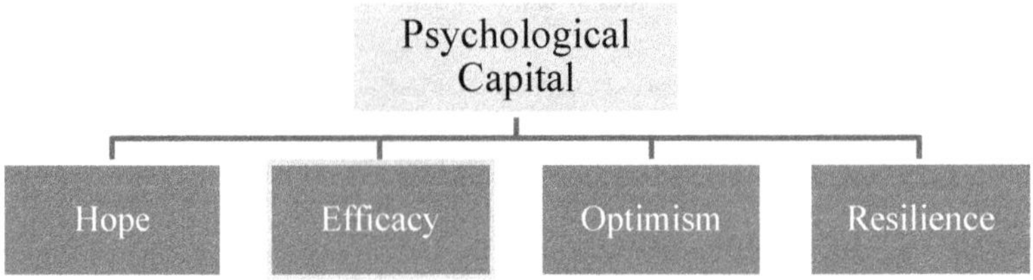

Psychological Capital and Related Studies

Positive psychology has introduced the concept of psychological capital as a parallel term with the traditional economic capital, human capital and social capital (Manheim, 2011). Several studies have examined the role of psychological capital (PsyCap) in fostering positive organizational climate and work outcomes. However, there were very few investigations on the benefits of PsyCap in academic settings. Datu et al., (2018) assessed the extent to which teachers' PsyCap can be associated with optimal academic and well-being outcomes of students. On the basis of the data from 606 Filipino high school students who studied with teachers of different level of PsyCap, the results of structural equation modeling revealed that teachers' PsyCap positively predicted academic engagement, academic performance, flourishing, interdependent happiness, and positive affect of the students. Implications of the findings are elaborated in terms of how teachers' PsyCap can potentially assist in facilitating positive student outcomes in a non-Western context.

Wang, Chen, and Hsu (2014) examined the role of teachers' Psychological capital on the teaching effectiveness in the elementary schools of Taiwan. They have reported that teachers with higher level of psychological capital use more positive approaches to promote good classroom leadership, create a harmonious atmosphere for learning, carry out highly compatible teacher-student interaction, and become actively caring to motivate students to positive behavior. They also strongly influence students' academic achievement and help the students for learning. In fact, they are found to strongly influence students' thoughts, concepts, behavior, and learning.

Datu et al., (2018) examined how teachers' PsyCap is associated with students' academic motivation, engagement, and achievement using both cross-sectional and longitudinal approaches. Results of the cross-sectional study revealed that teachers' PsyCap was associated with higher autonomous motivation and controlled motivation of students even after controlling for relevant demographic variables. Longitudinal study showed that teachers' PsyCap was both a concurrent and prospective predictor of students' autonomous motivation, controlled motivation, academic engagement, and academic achievement even after controlling their respective auto-regressors and other relevant covariates.

Liu et al., (2015) reported a study on the mediating relationship between students' negative life events and teachers PsyCap with nursing students in China. They have observed that students' negative life events were negatively associated with the dimensions of school adjustment such as adaptation to interpersonal relationship, learning adaptation, campus life adaptation, career adaptation, emotional adaptation, self-adaptation, and degree of satisfaction. When these students were kept under the care of teacher with strong PsyCap as proctors, all their dimensions of school adjustment significantly improved. It was concluded in the research that teachers PsyCap partially mediated the relationship between students' negative life events and school adjustment.

Riolli et al., (2012) examined the role teachers' PsyCap as a buffer to undergraduate student stress. The sample consisted of undergraduate student assigned to teachers with different level of PsyCap as their proctors and academic mentor. Teachers' psychological capital was hypothesized to empower students with the necessary metal strength to cope up with adverse circumstances. Among undergraduate students from a university in the Western US, it was found that teachers PsyCap mediated between students stress and indices of psychological and physical well-being. In the case of psychological symptoms and health problems, teacher PsyCap buffered the impact of stress so that the relationship between stress and negative outcomes was reduced. In the case of satisfaction with life, teachers' PsyCap augmented a positive psychological outcome among the students. They have discussed implications for research on resilience to students' academic stress, the power of the teacher PsyCap to help the development of positive psychological outcomes in a variety of student situations, and implications for educators in developing and promoting positive outcomes based on this valuable personal capital of the teachers.

Although few studied are available on the impact of teachers PsyCap on students' life, performance, mental health, wellbeing and empowerment, all those studies are quite assuring about the significance of teachers PsyCap on students life. Hence, in the present research it is also proposed to examine and explain the PsyCap of the women primary teachers in Odisha so that some knowledge can be gained about their level in the four areas of the PsyCap and necessary guideline can be provided to the school administration.

Rationale for the Study

Cited in the review of literature, several studies have pointed out that teachers' psychosocial attributes are significant sources of students' all-round development. Teacher-student relationship, particularly during school years, is not only an academic contract, but is more a socio-emotional interaction. It is always found that experiences in the school have lasting impact on the academic success and personality development of every individual. Hence, knowledge about the teachers' relevant psychosocial attributes, particularly of the primary school teachers in Odisha, would definitely be a source of guidance not only to teachers but also to all those people including the local, district and state administration, who are part of primary education in Odisha. Rural people are actually the backbone of Odisha because 80% of the population lives in rural part of Odisha. Therefore, the present study was undertaken to make a general assessment of the teacher related psychosocial attributes in rural Odisha. Further, as the women teachers constitute a majority of the teacher population in the primary schools of Odisha, the present study was proposed to concentrate on women teachers only.

Although, various approaches to understand the psychosocial attributes of effective teachers have been discussed in the review of literature, Chatopadhyay's psychosocial competence scale was used in the present study for its relevance to the culture of Odisha.

Similarly, several studies cited in the literature have also provided evidences about the importance of teachers' PsyCap for their teacher effectiveness. Therefore, it was also undertaken in the present study to examine the nature of the four PsyCap variables among the women primary teachers. To measure the four PsyCaps of the teachers, Adult PsyCaps Scale developed by the Positive Psychology Center, University Pennsylvania, was used because a revised format of the test in the context of teachers was available. Further, the teacher effectiveness relating to the Walker's constructs are examined in the study to provide a general estimate of the teacher effectiveness among the women primary teachers in Odisha and also to find out from a theoretical perspective, how psychosocial attributes and psychological capitals affect the teacher effectiveness. Further, several prior studies have examined the impact of ethnicity, marital status, school administration, financial incentives, school environment, and community support on teacher effectiveness. Teachers' level of education and experience has also been discussed in the literature as significant factors of teacher effectiveness. Hence, it was also undertaken in the present study to examine the group differences among the teachers in respect of not only teacher effectiveness but also in psychosocial attributes and psychological capital.

Arising from the above rationale, the following major objectives were formulated for the study.

Objectives of the Study

Arising from the above review of literature and purpose of the study, the following objectives were developed for the present research.

i. To find out and explain in general about the characteristics and strength of each of the Chatopadhyay's psychosocial attributes outlined for teacher effectiveness among the women primary teachers in Odisha.

ii. To find out and explain the impact of level of experience and level of education on each of the Chatopadhyay's psychosocial attributes from six groups of women teachers with varying level of education and experience.

iii. To find out and also explain in general about the characteristics and strength of each of the four psychological capital among the women primary teachers in Odisha.

iv. To find out and explain the impact of level of experience and level of education on each of the psychological capital from six groups of women teachers with varying level of education and experience.

v. To study the effectiveness of the women teachers in Odisha in general with respect to each of the ten Walker's teacher effectiveness characteristics.

vi. To examine differences in teacher effectiveness characteristics among groups having different levels of education and teaching experience.

vii. To find out by regression analyses how teacher effectiveness variables are predicted and explained by the psychosocial attributes of the teachers.

viii. To find out by regression analyses how teacher effectiveness variables are predicted and explained by the PsyCap variables of the teachers.

Hypotheses.

(i) Teachers with higher level of education will be stronger in all the positive psychosocial attributes and will be less punishing and less superstitious.

(ii) Teachers with more experience will be stronger in all the positive psychosocial attributes and will be less punishing and less superstitious.

(iii) Teachers with higher level of education will have better PsyCap.

(iv) Teachers with more experience will have better PsyCap.

(v) Teachers with higher level of education will be more effective teachers.

(vi) Teachers with higher level of experience will be more effective teachers.

(vii) Psychosocial attributes of teachers will significantly predict their teacher effectiveness

(viii) PsyCap variables of teachers will significantly predict their teacher effectiveness.

Chapter III

Method of Study

This section presents the design of the study, locale of the study, participants and their socio-demographic characteristics, description of the tests and the considerations that guided the selection of the tests, and finally, the procedure of data collection.

Sample

The participants of the present study were 420 women primary school teachers of the state of Odisha who were selected from 128 schools of six different districts including coastal, western, northern and southern parts of the state. Out of these 420 teachers who were selected from a population of approximately 1500 primary teachers for the present study, 210 teachers had the educational qualification of graduation and above, where as the remaining 210, had the qualification of intermediate and less. Each of these two groups again was divided into 3 subgroups having three different levels of service experience, i.e., experience of less than 5 years, between 15 to 20 years and above 30 years with 70 teachers in each group. The method of sampling may be designated as purposive random sampling. Maximum care was taken to make the sample representative of the population. A schematic representation of the sample design of the study is given below.

Sample Design

Experience Education	<5 yrs.	15-20 yrs.	> 30 yrs.	Total Sample Size
Graduate & above	70	70	70	
Intermediate and below	70	70	70	420

The selected teachers represented from different communities like general caste, schedule caste, schedule tribe, and other back ward classes. Because the study was proposed to be carried out on rural primary school teachers, 315 upgraded primary schools were identified where teaching facilities up to class VIII are available. The schools were chosen from the rural areas of the districts. Although, all demographic variables are not controlled in the sample selection, nearly equal numbers of teachers were selected from different communities. With regard to marital status of the teachers, 386 teachers were married and 323 of them had one or more children. Most of the teachers commute daily from 5 to 60 kilometers from their home to school. All the selected schools are government schools where the medium of instruction is Odia, the language of the state. All the schools are very old schools having around 200 and more student strength including both boys and girls and about 4 to 6 teachers. Most of the schools have adequate infrastructure and building. The schools are managed by a local body called the 'Village Committee' which includes parents and significant people of the locality. The usual school time is 10AM to 4PM, although the time schedule changes during the summer. The schools are under the administrative control of the Department of School and Mass Education, Government of Odisha. All the schools were found to have satisfactory results of the students, and low dropout rate during the past ten years. Each school has an experienced teacher as the head master to manage the school administration.

Scales and Measures

Three different measures were used in the present study namely; the Chatopadhyay's scale of psychosocial attributes, Adult psychological capital scales of Positive Psychology Center, and Walker's scale of teacher effectiveness. These measures are all standardized tests which are described below.

Chatopadhyay's scale of psychosocial attributes. The scale measures 10 psychosocial attributes of the teachers namely; self image, locus of control, listening profile, empathetic ability, sensitivity profile, sense of humor, punishing behavior, ethical and moral values, superstition, and flow mindset. This scale was developed by Chatopadhyay (2014) and was validated on primary and secondary school teachers in West Bengal.

In total, the scale consists of 80 items in the form of statements to be asked to a teacher. There are eight items to evaluate each of the psychosocial attributes. For a statement, the teacher is required to evaluate herself in respect of her opinion, attitude, behavior and conviction in a four point scale from 0 to 3 depending on the nature of the statement. For example, there is a statement in the scale, "There is a direct connection between how hard the students study and the grades they get". Here the teacher is supposed to give her opinion. If she strongly agrees with statement, she gets a score of '3' in internal locus of control. On the other hand, if strongly disagrees with the statement, she gets a score of '0' in internal locus of control and if she believes something in between, she either gets a score of '1' or '2'.

Similarly, for the statement in the scale, "I feel relaxed when I talk with my students'" she evaluates her feeling of relaxation. When she feels that she is highly relaxed talking with students, she assigns herself a score of '3' and if she does not feel relaxed at all, she assigns herself a score of '0'. Likewise, for different items in the test, the nature and perspective of evaluation of the statement are different. Therefore, only the following general instructions were given to the teachers, and the researcher provided guidance to the teachers during data collection when they required understanding a statement.

Instruction: In this questionnaire different statements are given relating to the behavior, believes, feelings, attitudes and convictions of teachers and you as a teacher rate every statement only at one point out of the four. Your evaluation will be used for research purpose only and it will be kept strictly confidential. So, read each statement attentively and evaluate the same genuinely.

For each of the 10 psychosocial attributes, the items in the scale are randomly distributed. As there are 8 items for each attribute, the maximum score for any psychosocial attribute is 24. There are also reverse scoring for some of the items in the scale which have been identified in the scoring key. The scale is also used by other researchers in India for educational researches. The items in the scale were also translated into Odia language to help the teachers appropriately understand the contents of the statement because many of the primary teachers are very good in English. The scale is presented in Appendix-1.

Adult psychological capital scale (Positive Psychology Center). Four personal resources constitute the psychological capital namely; self-efficacy, hope, optimism and resilience. In the present study, each of these aspects of PsyCap was measured on the basis of teachers' responses to 8 items derived from Adult PsyCap Scale developed by the Positive Psychology Center, University Pennsylvania. The scale was used in the present study because the items were revised and modified to the cultural context of the teachers in Odisha (Dash, 2016). The items in the test are in the form of statements to which the teacher responds by his personal believes, attitudes and convictions on a four-point scale ranging from 0 to 3. For example, if a teacher completely agrees to an item, "I believe my students are competent learners", then she is assigned a score of '3' on optimism. On the other hand, if she completely disagrees with the statement, she is assigned a score of '0' on optimism. If she believes something in between, she is assigned a score of '1' or '2'. Similarly, for an item, "I am frequently worried about my health", if the teacher responds, 'yes, always', she gets a score of '0' on hope, and if she responds 'no, never', she gets a score of three on hope. Likewise, the responses of the teachers were collected on all 32 items in the test. The items relating to the four PsyCaps were randomly distributed in the scale. The items were clearly outlined in the scoring key for which reverse scoring was required. The maximum score for each PsyCap variable was 24.

Walker's teacher effectiveness scale. To measure the variables of teacher effectiveness, Walker's (2008) construct was used in the present study. On basis of his identifications of effective teacher characteristics, he has developed a short scale consisting of 60 items, 6 items measuring each of the 10 teacher effectiveness attributes. Each item is a statement to which the teacher responds on a five-point scale ranging from 0 to 4. The statements for different attributes of teacher effectiveness are randomly distributed along the scale. For example, "A teacher should have full confidence in the subject she teaches" is a statement in the scale relating to the teacher's preparedness. If the teacher totally agrees with the statement, she gets a score of '4' on preparedness and if totally disagrees with the statement; she gets a score of '0' on preparedness. Likewise, the scale has other points such as agree, uncertain, and disagree for which she respectively gets 3, 2, or 1on preparedness. Similarly, an item relating to personal concern of teachers is "Teachers should give proper time to the guardian for the solution of student's problem". If the teacher totally agrees with the statement, she gets a score of '4' and if she totally disagrees with the statement, she gets a score of

'0'. Hence, the maximum score for each of the teacher effectiveness attribute is 24. This scale has been widely used in educational researches on teacher effectiveness.

Procedure

All the three measures were finalized and typed by the researcher and two research assistants, (M. Phil. in Psychology).The research assistants were thoroughly familiarized with the administration of the tests, and helped the researcher in data collection.

First of all, the researcher visited the designated districts to apprise the administrative authorities of the schools about the purpose of the research and to avail permission for data collection from the women teachers of the schools. Then, she visited schools and apprised the headmasters of the schools and requested them to arrange their convenient time for data collection. The researcher planned the schedule of data collection district-wise, so that data collection could be completed in a district in about one month. It took about eight months for total data collection with the help of two research assistants.

All the teachers of a school selected to be included in the study, were at a time explained about the purpose of the research, about the tests and the way they were supposed to give their responses. They were also requested to write about their educational qualification, years of teaching experience, and other relevant personal information in the provided sheet. Although no time limit was fixed for the teachers to complete the test, usually they took $1^{1}/_{2}$ to 2 hours to complete all the three tests. Either the researcher or any one of the research assistants was present in a school during the data collection and whenever required they explained the contents of the statements to the teachers. The teachers were requested to be genuine while giving their response. In fact most of the teachers were very cooperative during the data collection. Then, all the data were organized and tabulated by the researcher with the help of the research assistants. Finally, the data were statistically analyzed by using the SPSS.

Chapter IV

Results and Discussion

The results and discussions of the present study are organized in three parts (i) relating to the psychosocial attributes, (ii) relating to the psychological capital, and (iii) relating to the teacher effectiveness of the women primary teachers in Odisha. For each of these attributes results and discussions are presented in two levels. In the first place, the state of affairs of women primary teachers in general relating to the above attributes are presented and discussed. Then, following a 2 (Level of education: graduate and above, intermediate and below) x 3 (Level of experience: <5 years, 15-20 years, >30 years) factorial design, groups differences in respect of each of the attributes are analyzed and discussed. Finally, some suggestions are presented for developing awareness and providing counseling to the teachers who are deficient in any of the attributes or skills to become effective teachers.

Psychosocial Attributes of Women Primary Teachers in Odisha

The ten psychosocial attributes (8 positive and 2 negative) of the women teachers relating to the Chatopadhyay (2014) measures were examined following a 2 (Level of education: graduate and above, intermediate and below) x 3 (Level of experience: <5 years, 15-20 years, >30 years factorial design. In the first place, the combined means and standard deviations of each of the ten attributes for all the six groups of subjects were computed to bring out a general assessment of the women teachers' psychosocial attributes. The group means, standard deviations, combined means, and combined standard deviations for the ten psychosocial attributes are reported in Table 1. The combined means of the eight positive attributes are presented in Figure 1 and of the two negative attributes are presented in Figure 2.

(i) General assessment of psychosocial attributes. On the basis of the combined means and combined standard deviations of each of the ten psychosocial attributes (Table 1), it was found women teachers were very good in Empathetic Ability with a mean of 17.07 and standard deviation of 3.00. Out of a maximum score of 24, they are said to have more than 70% of empathetic ability on the average which according to the Chattopadhyaya's norm (Excellent: 71% to 90% Outstanding: Above 90%) is an excellent skill among the women teachers. According to many prior studies (e.g., Deiro, 1996; Garrison & Liston, 2004; Butler, 2012) empathetic ability is one of the best gift of teachers which brings the students and the teachers into emotional proximity. Deiro (1996) concluded that teachers who lack in empathetic ability are perceived by the students with fear and anger while teachers with high empathetic ability are perceived by them with love and affection. According to Garriston and Liston (2004) an empathetic teacher gives each student a framework to build on, in which all his /her thoughts, opinions, and feelings are smoothened. They further reported that teachers cannot expect to have an impact on intellectual development of students without becoming involved in their emotional processes and empathy is the best emotional transaction between the teacher and students. Butler (2012) reported that empathetic teachers set up students to deepen relationships with their classmates and people that they know outside of school. Mother Teresa has once remarked that empathy for children make them more understanding and empower them to fight back in their life. Hence, empathy is a great skill of the teachers as well as of the students. Arising from this study, it is highly assuring that the women primary teachers in Odisha are abundant in empathy which is a strong positive sign among them to be effective teachers for students of primary education in Odisha. These teachers need to be appreciated by the school administration for this great virtue with them.

Another important psychosocial attribute found very good among the women primary teachers of Odisha is their Listening Profile. The combined mean for this attribute is 15.80 and the combined standard deviation is only 2.37. Similarly, out of a maximum score of 24, the women teachers' ability is 65.83% which according to the norm is a very good listening skill of the teachers (Very Good: 61% to 70%). Many prior studies have also reported that teachers, who patiently listen to their students' problem, share their experiences with them, assure them of their ability in learning and express their concern and belief in them, become the most favorite teachers (e. g., Butler, 2012; Hargreaves, 2012; Hudson, 2017). Butler (2012) compared the performance of students under high and proactively listening teachers, high but reactively listening teachers and teachers with poor listening ability. He observed that college students performed best under proactively listening teachers; and even they performed better under reactively listening teachers than under teachers with indifference or poor listening ability. Hargreaves (2012) reported from a study that listening is the most powerful tool of a teacher which helps the teacher to learn who the students are and to find out what sparks their curiosity. He also reported that teacher's listening has a strong motivating power for both student and the teacher in the class. Teachers who engage part of their classroom time listening to students become more motivated to take classes and students become more willing to attend to their classes than teachers who only teach in the class without listening to the students. Hudson (2017) has reported five reasons why listening is important for teachers. According to him teacher's listening to students make the students feel respected, motivate them for study, and help them to develop self-confidence. It also helps the teacher to find out what is really going on with the students, to provide an effective role model to students, and to get appropriate feedback from parents. Hence, arising from the results of the present study, it is extremely assuring that the women primary teachers in Odisha have a very good listening profile which would be strongly supportive for a quality primary education in Odisha.

Ethical and moral values are the other important attributes in which the women teachers are found to be very good. The combined means on this attribute is also 15.80 and the combined standard deviation is only 3.12. Hence, on the average, women teachers are said to have 65.83% of ability in this attribute (Very Good: 61% to 70%). Many prior studied have reported the significance of teacher's ethical and moral values in the life of the students (e.g., Cambell, Kyriakides, Muijs, & Robinson, 2003; Pantic &Wubbels, 2012). Pantic and Wubbels (2012) examined how teacher's ethical and moral values have influenced the student-teacher relationship in term of level of control and affiliation, students' relationship with parents, peers and students cultural competence. They have reported that when students perceived their teacher as ethical and moral, they had a strong affiliation for that teacher and they were easily managed and controlled by the teacher in his / her class room. The students respond to the teacher with grace and respect. On the other hand, when students perceived their teachers as unethical, partial, and discriminating, some of the students reacted implicitly while others reacted violently. Students do not show affiliation to such teachers and those teachers lack adequate control in the class room. They have also reported that such behavior of the students even generalized to their relationships with parents, peers and other relationships. In the behavior analysis of students who complained about their teachers as unethical and discriminating, they found that those students were more aggressive towards their parents and peers. Cambell et al., (2004) in a study on the impact of teachers' moral behavior on students reported that teachers are the most significant sources of moral and emotional development of students helping them to overcome shame and distrust, and also disillusionment and depression. Hence, it is further assuring that the women primary teachers in Odisha having a very good sense of ethical and moral values are a strong support system for a positive and quality education in the primary schools of Odisha.

The Sensitivity Profile of the teachers is also found to be very good with a combined mean of 15.05 and standard deviation of 4.11. Out of a maximum score of 24, the skill is said to be 62.7% (Very Good: 61% to 70%) on the average. But a relatively high standard deviation point to the fact that with respect to sensitivity profile, there is a wide gap among the teachers. While some of the teachers are very good or even excellent in the skill, others are poor. Several prior studies have also reported on the significance of teachers' sensitivity to teacher effectiveness. Bush, Caldwell, & Shakleford (2016) defined teachers' sensitivity as the ability of the teacher to respond consistently and effectively in addressing to students' questions, concerns and needs. Teaching sensitively includes the awareness of the teachers about individual students' academic, social, emotional and cultural needs in a way that allows them to anticipate the areas of difficulty for the student and thereby, provide appropriate and effective learning opportunities and levels of support for all students in the classroom. They have reported that with teachers of high sensitivity, students significantly progress when learning opportunities are academically and developmentally appropriate but challenging. When a teacher shows sensitivity, students view that teacher as a source of support, guidance, and reassurance. Teaching sensitively promotes trust and students feel comfortable sharing their ideas, taking risks, and challenging themselves academically, socially and emotionally. It also allows students to work comfortably on their own and in groups because they know they can approach the teacher and s/he will be helpful. However, although it is assuring that women primary teachers in Odisha have a very good sensitivity profile on the average, but a large segment of teachers are also not good in the skill. Hence, it may be suggested from the results of this research that definite awareness and training programs should be undertaken in the teacher education curriculum to improve the sensitivity profile of the women primary teachers in Odisha who are not good in the skill.

The attribute on which the women teachers have the next highest combined mean is flow mind set. The combined mean is 13.47 and combined standard deviation is 3.34. Out of a maximum score of 24, the average ability of the teachers in this skill is said to be good as per the Chatopadhyaya's standard of reference (Good: 51% to 60%). Several prior studies have examined the relationship between teachers' mindset and teacher effectiveness (e.g., Paul, 2013; Bread & Hoy, 2010). Flow mindset of a teacher is defined by Bread and Hoy (2010) as a holistic sensation that the teachers feel when they act with total involvement` in a given class. Smith and Holy also described the flow mind set of teachers when their consciousness is harmoniously ordered, and they want to pursue teaching for the sake of teaching. Smith and Holy identified dimensions of teachers' flow mindset as perception of clear goals, challenge-skill balance, unambiguous feedback, sense of control, and concentration on the task at hand. In their study on 521 teachers from elementary, middle and high schools, they reported that in the class of teachers with flow mindset, students are more personally motivated to succeed, more actively engaged in learning, and communicate better with peers than under teachers with fixed mindset. They also observed that flow mind set of the teachers encourages higher order thinking, genuineness, and learner-centered beliefs among the students. Paul (2013) observed that in classes of teachers with flow mind set, there is more engagement, more respect for self and others, fewer resistant behaviors, greater non-directivity (student-initiated and student-generated activities), and greater student achievement. Paul also reported in the study that most of the students who do not wish to come to school or who dislike school do so primarily because they dislike their teacher having a fixed mindset. Similarly, Bread and Hoy (2010) observed that growing interest in teaching helps the teacher to develop a flow mindset and such teachers help the students to reflect on an increasing awareness that richer and deeper learning can flow from having them to struggle with a challenging task and persist until completion. Students in the class of the teachers with flow mindset learn to positively explain and accept their failure and grow up beyond it. Bread and Hoy also observed that teachers with flow mind set demonstrate greater confidence on their students and believe that struggle is the best way for achievement and success and a sense of invulnerability among students is mostly created by teachers with flow mindset.

Evidences were also reported that significant learning benefits result when students are allowed to do some of the hard works on their own and struggle with ideas they do not quite yet understand. It is evident from the above discussions that teachers flow mind set is a significant source of teacher effectiveness. It is extremely assuring that the women teachers in the primary schools of Odisha have a good flow mind set on the average. But it can be said that being a very important teacher skill, it has to be still better. On the other hand, a combined standard deviation of 3.34 is quite high to suggest that there are also large numbers of teachers who are poor in this attribute. Hence, it is suggested from this research that awareness and counseling programs should be undertaken to help the teachers change from fixed to flow mindset so that the students in the primary schools of Odisha get better quality of education.

Sense of humor is a very significant teacher attribute to help teacher effectiveness. The combined mean of the women primary teachers in this attribute is 13.40 and the combined standard deviation is 3.86. Hence, although on the average, this attribute is found to be good among the teachers, a high standard deviation point to the fact that many of those teachers are severely lacking in this attribute of teacher effectiveness. Many prior studies have reported on the significance of this attribute on teacher effectiveness (e.g., Bacay, 2006; Lovorn, 2008). Bacay (2006) reported from a study on college students that humor can play an important role in today's college classrooms as it has a humanizing effect on the students resulting from the image of the teacher. It has also physiological, psychological, social and cognitive (educational) benefits for the students. Some of these physiological benefits observed in the study of students include better muscle relaxation, stimulated circulation, improved respiration, and exercise of lung and chest muscles, increased production of body's natural pain killers called endorphins, as well as lowered pulse rate and blood pressure. He also reported that humor is a psychological tool that helped students cope with fear and stress, enhance their sense of well-being, boost their self-image, self-esteem, self-confidence, as well as alleviated their anxiety and depression. Similarly, Lovorn (2008) reported from a study of college students that although humor is not an essential teaching tool in classrooms, it has been found that teachers with high multiple intelligences usually use humor as a teaching tool. Humor coupled with the use of analogy and metaphor provided students with added positive associations and they more actively processed and remembered the information. He also observed that humor can be used as a powerful tool to put students at ease and make their overall learning process more enjoyable. This can be achieved when teachers integrate humor with content and use both planned and spontaneous humor. Humor can also be planned and executed to hold the students' attention and sustain a level of enjoyment that can facilitate learning.

Learning is a serious activity, but a sense of humor can go a long way toward making learning easier by decreasing tension in the classroom situations. Having a sense of humor is an indication that the teacher is human and can share with the group. Arising from these discussions, it may be concluded that sense of humor is a grand attribute of teacher effectiveness. However, although the women primary teachers in Odisha are found to have a good sense of humor on the average, the large value of standard deviation point out that there are many teachers who also severely lack in this skill.

Further, as children in primary schools are small children, an understanding of age-appropriate sense of humor by the teachers is very essential. Hence, it is suggested from the findings of the present research that teachers should properly motivated and trained to learn the strategies to use age-appropriate sense of humor in the primary classrooms so that students get a lot benefit not only for their academic skills but also for their socio-emotional development.

Self-image is a very important psychosocial attribute of an effective teacher which has been extensively pointed out in the research literature. In the present study, the combined mean of self-image is found to be 12.44 and the combined standard deviation as 2.86. Hence, out a maximum score of 24, the attribute has an average of 51.83% among the women primary teachers of Odisha which is just good enough as per the Chattopadhyay's norm. However, the standard deviation of 2.45 points to the fact that many women primary teachers have also poor self-image. Prior studies which examined the relationships between teachers' self-image and teacher effectiveness have reported strong correlations between these two variables (e.g., Gow & Kember, 2007; Gao& Liu, 2013; Walker, 2008). Walker (2008), who examined the self-image of 340 secondary school teachers on five attributes of self-image namely; global competence or subjective feeling of capability, physical self-concept, social evaluation, emotionality-rationality, and intellectual self-concept, observed that each of these attributes significantly correlates with teacher effectiveness. Social evaluation has the highest correlation followed by emotionality-rationality, global competence, intellectual self-concept and finally of physical self-concept. Gao and Liu reported from a study of 275 primary and secondary school teachers that there is a strong relationship between teachers self-image and the four factors of teacher effectiveness namely; teacher as an individual, teacher as a curriculum designer and manager, teacher as a teacher-student interaction motivator, and teacher as an innovator. They have reported that a positive global self-image is found to have consistently improved the teacher effectiveness. On the other hand, Gow and Kember (2007) reported that teachers who have a poor self-image have very low job satisfaction, have least interaction with students and colleagues, and easily pick up troubles with students. Students' perceptions of these teachers are marked by a feeling of disrespect and hesitation. The above findings from research clearly pointed to importance teachers' self-image for their effectiveness as teachers. Although, the self-image of women prime teachers in Odisha seems to be good on the average, most of them are likely to have low self-image which is really a matter of concern. Hence, it is suggested that appropriate counseling programs should be developed to boost the self-image of the women primary teachers in Odisha during their in-service teachers' training programs.

Rose and Medway (1981) examined teacher locus of control and student achievement on several standardized tests. The results indicated that both male and female students, regardless of their locus of control, gained more on the achievement measures under internal teachers than under external teachers. Gaziel (2008) provided related evidence that internal teachers had helped better student achievement than external teachers. This research found that internal teachers took a more active role in the instructional process and consequently positively influence students' performance. Several other studies have also examined the relation between locus of control and teacher characteristics (Richardson, 2001; Rose & Medway, 1993). Richardson (1987) reported that internal teachers were more likely to implement successful innovative techniques and motivate students. While examining the teacher variables of age, gender, and race, he indicated that internality increased with age and the females teachers appeared to be more internally controlled than males. Richardson maintained that young teachers because of their lack of experience may be overly concerned about issues critical to their successful classroom functioning. All these findings from research point to the internal locus of control as a significant attribute of teacher effectiveness.

It is observed in the findings of the present research that the combined mean of internal locus of control for all groups of teachers is only 11.44 and the combined standard deviation is 2.47. Hence, out of a maximum score of 24, the average of internality among the women teachers is only 47.66% which is poor according to the Chatopadhyay's standard of reference (poor: 41 to 50 %). Further the standard deviation of 2.47 points to the fact that there are many teachers who are strongly externals. Here, it may be pointed out that by socio-cultural exigencies; women in Odisha have a strong faith in God, fate, horoscope and so on and therefore, they are more likely to be externals. Hence, it is matter of concern and appropriate counseling programs should be provided to women primary teachers of Odisha to help them develop internality in their professional attitudes so that they become effective primary teachers. The above discussions about the positive psychosocial attributes of women primary teachers in Odisha pointed out that they are quite good in some of the attributes like empathy, listening profile, ethical and moral values and sensitivity profile while in some others, they are not as good as it is required. Hence, arising out of this research, some suggestions are provided for training and counseling of those teachers.

The above discussions explained about the positive psychosocial attributes of the women primary teachers in Odisha. Data were also collected about two negative attributes namely punishing behavior and superstition. Generally punishment in schools seems to be ineffective and unacceptable method of controlling and maintaining behavior and discipline as it brings negative rather than positive consequences in the whole process of teaching and learning. Physical punishment seems to increase child's aggression, increase antisocial behavior, lower intellectual achievements, enhance poor quality of teacher student relation and cause mental health problem (Arif & Rafi (2007)). Since punishment tend to de-humanize children and make them feel scared, ashamed and worthless during learning and teaching process, it is better to be eliminated in both homes and schools so as to enhance positive learning (Cicognani, 2004). It should be also abolished because it is interfering with students' right to be treated with dignity and as a result is interfering with their right to a quality education. In the present study, it is found that the combined mean about punishing behavior among the women primary teachers in Odisha is 13.34 with a combined standard deviation of 3.71. Out of a maximum score of 24, there is about 55.58% of punishing behavior among the women primary teachers which is definitely high and is a matter of concern. Further, a high standard deviation also point out that there are many teachers who are very highly punishing to students although there are also many teachers who are less punishing. It may be pointed out that although schools in Odisha have been declared as punishment free zones, it's not appropriately functioning in the primary schools of Odisha. Hence, it is extremely pertinent that teachers' training and counseling programs should be carried out in the state to help the teachers to be aware about the negative consequences of punishment to students and also provide guideline to teachers as how to deal with students' problems in the school and in the classroom.

Another important negative psychosocial attribute relevant to teachers in Odisha is about their superstition. Notwithstanding increased literacy rate, superstition continues to grip minds of people in the hinterland of Odisha and one study revealed that many rural and tribal teachers are no exception to these superstitious beliefs. Sharma (2010) carrying out an extensive study reported that teachers' superstition very strongly and negatively influence the students' self-image, self-regulation, scientific attitude, interest, creativity, sensitivity and scientific temper. Other studies have also reported that students are more attracted to teachers who communicate superstitious believes which negatively influence their behavioral autonomy and academic performance. In the present study, it is found that the combined mean for superstition of women primary teachers in Odisha is 11.65 with a combined standard deviation of 2.23. Around a 48.54% of superstitious believes among the teachers is definitely not a good sign for quality education of students and particularly in the development of students. Furthermore, a relatively low value of standard deviation point to the fact that many of the women primary teachers in Odisha are actually superstitious. Hence, it is suggested that appropriate training and counseling services should be provided to help the teachers get over their superstitious believe and appropriately guide the students to develop their scientific temperament and thinking.

Table 1

Means and Standard Deviations, combined means and combined standard deviations of Psychosocial Attributes of Graduate and Intermediate Teachers for Three Levels of Teaching Experience

Education		Graduates & Post Graduates			Intermediates & Matriculates			Combined Mead & SD
Level of Experience		<5 yrs.	15-20 yrs.	< 30 yrs.	<5 yrs.	15-20 yrs.	>30 yrs.	
self-Image (24)	Mean	11.23	14.11	14.17	9.35	12.66	13.09	12.44
	SD	2.14	3.11	2.37	2.28	2.54	2.27	2.86
Locus of control(int.) (24)	Mean	8.57	13.43	14.61	8.95	11.76	11.31	11.44
	SD	1.58	2.23	2.14	2.09	2.71	2.45	2.47
Listening profile (24)	Mean	12.63	15.57	19.12	12.18	15.97	19.35	15.80
	SD	2.67	2.18	2.54	2.36	3.12	2.21	2.37
Empathetic ability (24)	Mean	14.32	18.19	20.21	14.54	16.71	18.45	17.07
	SD	2.46	2.83	3.61	3.49	2.58	2.06	3.00
Sensitivity profile (24)	Mean	11.26	16.39	18.14	10.36	16.37	17.78	15.05
	SD	4.28	3.91	3.84	3.45	3.77	4.53	4.11
Sense of humor (24)	Mean	10.36	14.19	15.17	10.87	13.93	15.87	13.40
	SD	4.06	3.94	3.81	3.25	3.85	3.56	3.86
Punishing behavior (24)	Mean	17.22	12.56	10.31	16.98	12.43	10.51	13.34
	SD	3.44	4.29	3.16	3.57	3.46	2.87	3.71
Ethical / moral values (24)	Mean	12.24	15.68	19.45	12.44	16.07	18.93	15.80
	SD	2.45	3.08	3.19	2.73	2.54	3.17	3.12
Superstition (24)	Mean	11.37	11.29	12.22	12.13	11.77	11.24	11.65
	SD	1.57	1.91	2.43	1.28	2.10	3.26	2.23
Mindset (Flow) (24)	Mean	10.26	16.18	20.33	8.66	11.23	14.16	13.47
	SD	2.27	2.44	3.16	2.35	3.32	3.35	3.34

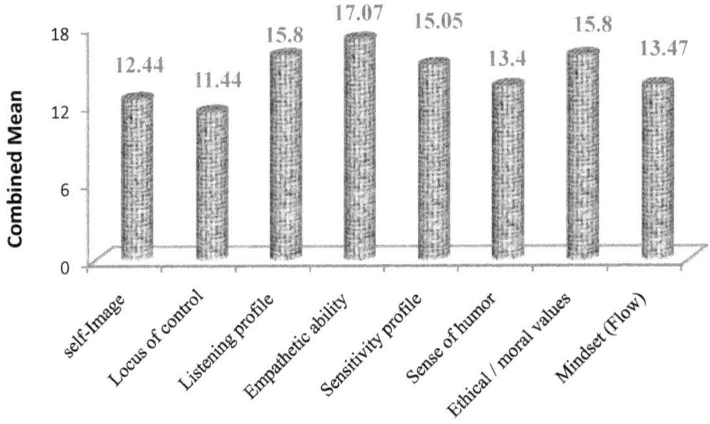

Figure 1. Combined mean for each of the eight positive psychosocial attributes

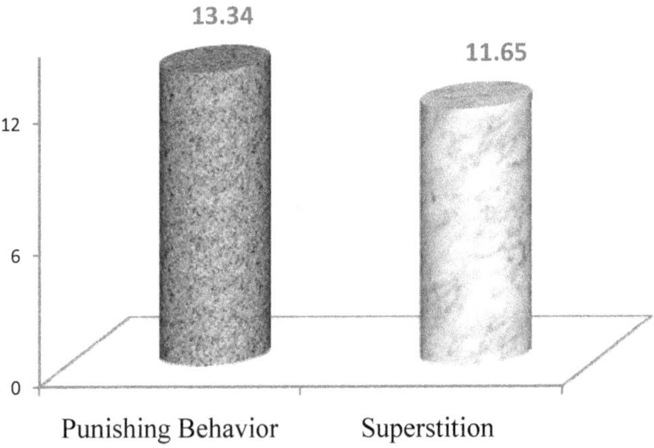

Figure 2. Combined mean for the two negative psychosocial attributes

Summary of the findings. The above findings may be summarized that women primary teachers in Odisha are excellent in empathetic ability, one of the most appreciated skills of teacher effectiveness. This teacher skill is more important for primary teachers of Odisha because it will help them check the dropout rate in primary schools which has been a matter of concern for primary education. Further, low combined standard deviation is also an indication that many of the teachers bear this quality and hence, the primary education in Odisha is in the hand of a lot of good teachers.

In other three positive attributes, in which the women teachers are found to be very good are their listening profile, sensitivity profile, and their ethical and moral values. Definitely, this is a very positive sign for the primary education in Odisha. But a larger value of standard deviation about sensitivity profile pointing to a 27% coefficient of variation (4.11 ÷ 15.05 x100 =27%) in the data definitely suggests that there are large numbers of teachers who don't have adequate sensitivity profile. This has probably resulted from the socio-cultural diversities like caste system and minorities and it is suggested that this aspects of the teachers should be addressed and taken care of by the administration for a better prospect in the primary education of Odisha.

In three of the positive attributes like self-image, sense of humor, and flow mindset, women teachers are just good enough on the average. But standard deviations and corresponding coefficients of variation are relatively high to suggest that there are large numbers of teachers who are grossly inadequate in these skills. For example, the coefficient of variation for self image is 23.00% (2.86÷12.44x100=23%), for sense of humor is 28.7% (3.86÷13.40x100=28.7%), and for flow mindset is 24.8% (3.34÷13.47x100=24.8%). Therefore, it is suggested that these attributes are also needed to be developed among the teachers by appropriate training and counseling. Finally, it is observed from the results that a large numbers of teachers are also external in locus of control which has been discussed in the literature as not good for teacher effectiveness. Hence, most of the teachers need to be guided to develop internal locus of control in their professional attitude.

On the other hand, many of the teachers are also high in the two negative attribute of teacher effectiveness namely; punishing behavior and superstition, which is not congenial for a good education of primary school children. Hence, counseling programs need to be developed to change these attitudes and behaviors among the women primary teachers for promoting better prospects in the primary education of Odisha.

(ii) Study of group differences in psychosocial attributes. From the general assessment of the teachers' psychosocial attributes, it was found that for many of the attributes, the combined standard deviations are quite high which suggest that there could be significant group differences among the six sub-groups of women teachers assigned in the present study following a 2 (Level of education: graduate and above, intermediate and below) x 3 (Level of experience: <5 years, 15-20 years, >30 years). Study of such group differences is essential to understand whether level of education and level of experience are significant factors contributing to the development of different psychosocial attributes of effective teachers. The results of two-way ANOVA including Tukey's HSD test for each of the 10 attributes are presented in Table 2 to Table 11. Graphs showing the means of different groups are also presented in Figure 1 to Figure 10.

Self-image. The results of analysis of variance and Tukey's HSD test for the self-image of teachers in different groups are presented in Table 2. It is observed from the results that the main effects of both level of education and level of experience are significant. The F-value for level of education is 54.25 [$F(1, 414) = 54.25$, $p < .01$] and for level of experience is 89.11[$F(2, 414) = 89.11$, $p < .01$]. The interaction effect between level of education and experience is not significant. The observation of the means as presented in Figure 1 a pointed out that for both graduate and intermediate teachers, there is a continuous improvement in the self-image from less than 5 years of experience to about 15 to 20 years of experience and after that the improvement stops. In Figure 1b, it also found that teachers with 5 years experience have distinctly lower self-image compared to teachers of both 20 and 30 years of experience. This difference is very clear for both graduate and intermediate teachers. However, to statistically corroborate these findings post hoc analyses of Tukey's HSD was carried out which showed that with same level of experience, graduate teachers have better self-image than the intermediate teachers. On the other hand, self-image is found to have improved for both intermediate and graduate teachers until around 20 years of experience and not beyond that. In the line of many prior studies, it may be concluded that higher academic qualification boosts the self-image of the teachers because of their better self-confidence. On the other hand, experience also helps improve the self-image of the teachers. However, beyond a certain level of experience, teachers acquire an optimal self-image for which they don't grow further. Therefore, it may suggested that higher qualification of teachers should always be given preference in the recruitment of teachers in the primary schools of Odisha and also experienced teachers should be uniformly assigned in different schools such that each school should have some experienced teachers.

Table 2

Results of Two way ANOVA (2: Level of Education X 3: Level of Experience) and Tukey's HSD test for Self-image of women teachers

Source	SS	df	MS	F
Level of Education (A)	334.72	1	334.72	54.25**
Level of Experience (B)	1099.62	2	549.81	89.11**
AXB	41.62	2	20.81	3.37
Error	2554.38	414	6.17	

Level of Education	Graduates & Post Graduates			Intermediates & Matriculates		
Level of Experience	<5 yrs.	15-20 yrs.	> 30 yrs.	<5 yrs.	15-20 yrs.	> 30 yrs.
Mean	11.23	14.11	14.17	9.35	12.66	13.09
	(1)	(2)	(3)	(4)	(5)	(6)
SD	2.63	2.87	2.54	1.98	2.45	2.88
Combined Mean (Edn.)	Graduates-13.17			Intermediates-11.70		
Combined Mean (Exp.)	<5 yrs.-10.29		15-20 yrs.-13.39		> 30 yrs.-13.63	
Significant mean differences inTukey's HSD Test:						
Level of Education	1 vs.4; 2 vs.5; 3vs. 6					
Level of Experience	1vs.2; 1vs.3; 4vs.5; 4vs.6					

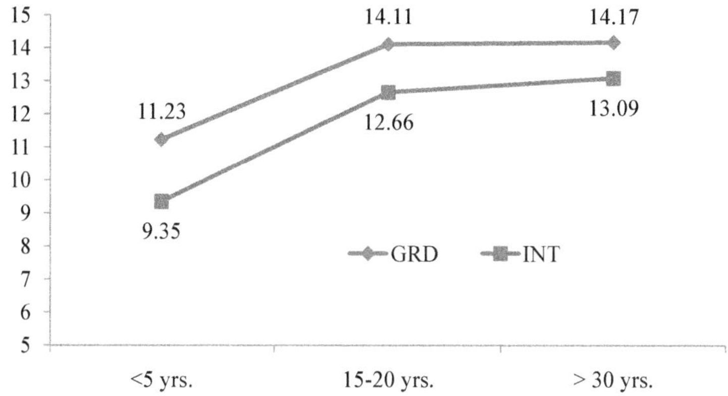

Figure 1a. Self-image of women teachers compared for level of education

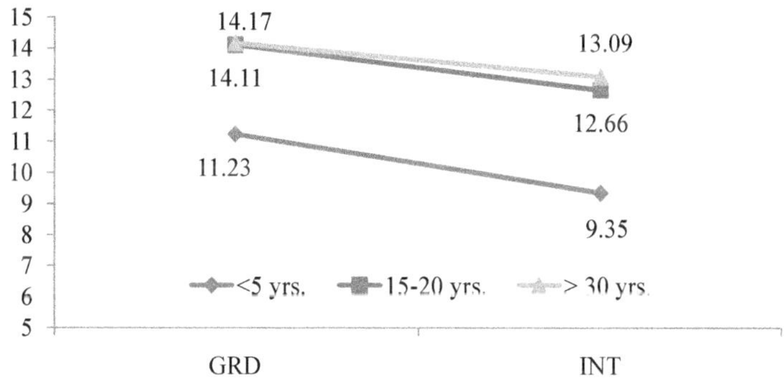

Figure 1b. Self-image of women teachers compared for level of experience

Locus of control. The result of analysis of variance and Tukey's test for internal locus of control are reported in Table 3 and the graphs relating to group means are presented in Figure 2a and 2b. The results of ANOVA pointed out that the main effect of level of education is significant [F (1, 414)

= 72.94, $p < .01$] and hence the graduate teachers are more internals compared to the intermediate teachers. However, it is observed from the results of Tukey's HSD test and also from the Figure 2a that at the 5 years level of experience, there is no significant difference in internal locus of control between graduate and intermediate teachers while the internality among both the groups of women teachers increased very rapidly until 20 years of experience in teaching and then, there is slow change in the internality of graduate teachers and no change in the internality of intermediate teachers. For this reason, the interaction effect between level of education and level of experience is also found to be significant [$F(2, 414) = 11.27$, $p < .01$]. On the other hand, the main effect of level of experience is also found significant [$F(2, 414) = 109.58$, $p < .01$] to point out that level of experience has also independent effect on the internal locus of control of the teachers. However, results of Tukey test on the level of experience point to some changes that while graduate teachers continue to develop internality across the span of their service career, intermediate teachers cease to change in internality after around 20 years of teaching. The finding is supportive to many prior studies that both education and experience help the teachers to be more internal and teachers with higher education continue to accept the process of change more than teachers with less education.

Table 3

Results of Two way ANOVA (2: Level of Education X 3: Level of Experience) and Tukey's HSD test for internal locus of control of women teachers

Source	SS	df	MS	F
Level of Education (A)	361.78	1	361.78	72.94**
Level of Experience (B)	1087.03	2	543.52	109.58**
AXB	110.80	2	55.90	11.27**
Error	2053.44	414	4.96	

Level of Education	Graduates & Post Graduates			Intermediates & Matriculates		
Level of Experience	<5 yrs.	15-20 yrs.	> 30 yrs.	<5 yrs.	15-20 yrs.	> 30 yrs.
Mean	8.57	13.43	14.61	8.95	11.76	11.31
	(1)	(2)	(3)	(4)	(5)	(6)
SD	1.94	2.38	2.41	1.75	2.08	2.36
Combined Mean (Edn.)	Graduates-12.20			Intermediates-10.67		
Combined Mean (Exp.)	<5 yrs.-8.76		15-20 yrs.-12.37		> 30 yrs.-12.96	
Significant mean differences inTukey's HSD Test:						
Level of Education	2 vs.5; 3vs. 6					
Level of Experience	1vs.2; 1vs.3; 2 vs.3; 4vs.5; 4vs.6					

Note:- * <.05; ** p<.01

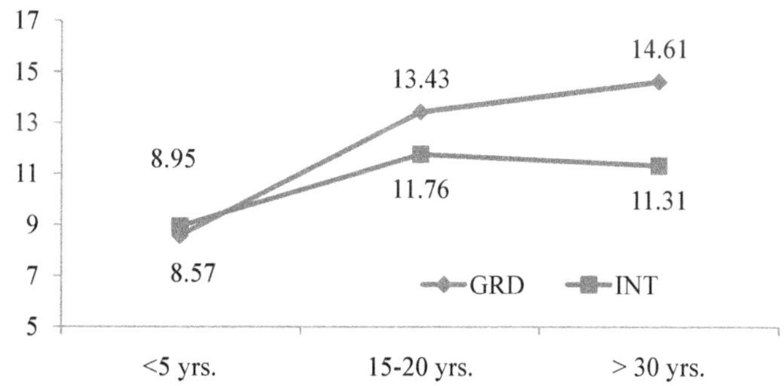

Figure 2a. Internal locus of control of women teachers compared for level of education

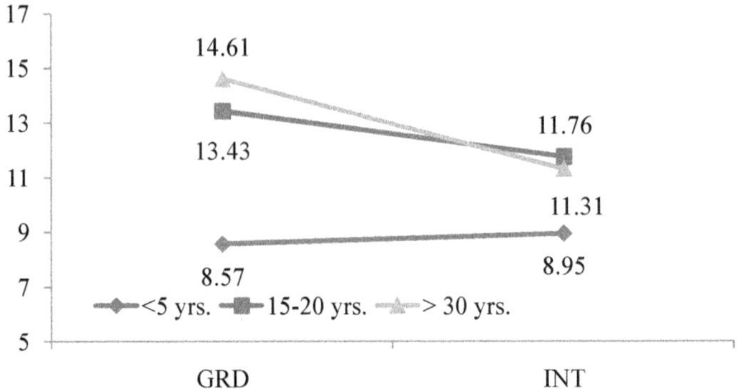

Figure 2b. Internal locus of control of women teachers compared for level of experience

Listening profile. The results of analysis of variance and Tukey's HSD test relating to listening profile are presented in Table 4 and the corresponding means are presented in Figure 3a and Figure 3b. It is observed in the results that the main effect of level of education is not significant [F (1, 414) = 2.17, p >.05] to conclude that listening profile as a teacher skill is not influenced by the level of education of the teacher, rather it is a basic personality skill of the teacher. On the other hand, the main effect of level of experience on listening profile of the teachers is found to be highly significant [F (2, 414) = 126.58, p <.01]. Such findings very clearly pointed out that experienced teachers become more and more sensitive to students issues and problems and they become more patient to listen and participate with students. In Figures 3a and 3b, it is clearly observed that for both groups of teachers, the listening profile is increasing steadily across the years of teaching and there are no visible differences in listening profile in respect of their educational qualifications. No interaction effect between level of education and level of experience was also observed with respect to the listening profile of the teachers. The findings of the present study correspond to the results of many prior studies that young teachers are usually reactive listeners and growing with experience they become more sensitive to students issues and become proactive listeners.

Table 4

Results of Two way ANOVA (2: Level of Education X 3: Level of Experience) and Tukey's HSD test for listening profile of women teachers

Source	SS	df	MS	F	
Level of Education (A)	22.18	1	22.18	2.17	
Level of Experience (B)	2587.30	2	1293.65	126.58**	
AXB	39.86	2	19.93	1.95	
Error	4231.08	414	10.22		
Level of Education	Graduates & Post Graduates			Intermediates & Matriculates	
Level of Experience	<5 yrs.	15-20 yrs.	> 30 yrs.	<5 yrs.	15-20 yrs.	> 30 yrs.

	<5 yrs.	15-20 yrs.	> 30 yrs.	<5 yrs.	15-20 yrs.	> 30 yrs.
Mean	12.63	15.57	19.12	12.18	15.97	19.35
	(1)	(2)	(3)	(4)	(5)	(6)
SD	3.17	3.78	3.54	4.36	3.72	3.81
Combined Mean (Edn.)	Graduates- 15.77			Intermediates-15.83		
Combined Mean (Exp.)	<5 yrs.-12.41		15-20 yrs.-15.77		> 30 yrs.-19.24	
Significant mean differences inTukey's HSD Test:						
Level of Education	Nil					
Level of Experience	1vs.2;1vs.3; 2 vs.3; 4vs.5; 4vs.6; 5vs.6					

Note:- * <.05; ** p<.01

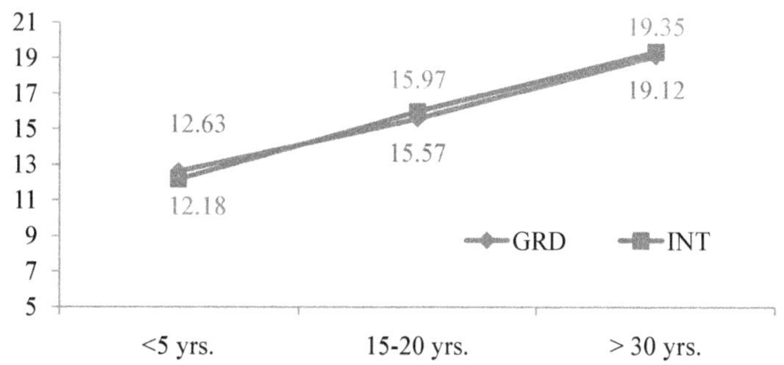

Figure 3 a. Listening profile of women teachers compared for level of education

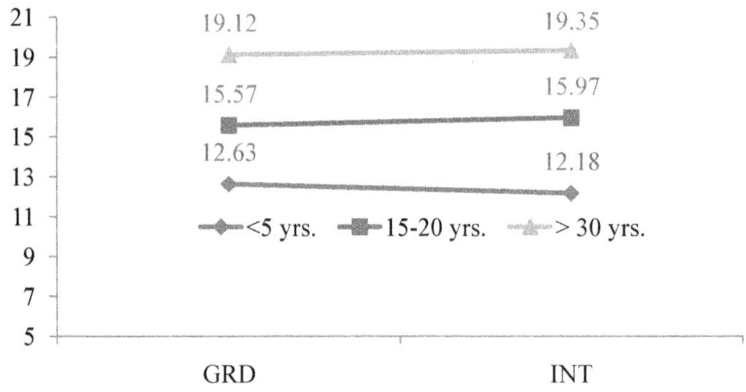

Figure 3b. Listening profile of women teachers compared for level of experience

Empathetic ability. This psychosocial attribute has been found to be the most prominent skill among the women primary teachers of Odisha. The result of analysis of variance and Tukey's HSD test for empathetic ability are presented in Table 5 and the graphs containing the corresponding means are presented in Figure 4a and 4b. The main effects of both level of education [F (1, 414) = 37.44, p <.01] and level of experience [F (2, 414) = 108.56, p <.01] are found to be significant while the interaction effect is not significant. From the results of Tukey's test and observation of the Figure 4a, it is found that intermediate teachers in the beginning of the career are not empathetically different from graduate teachers but as they continue with their teaching, both the groups grow up with empathetic skills; graduate teachers growing up faster in the skill than intermediate teachers. The findings may be explained with evidence from prior studies that experienced teachers gradually get more insight into students' problems and as a result, a strong bonding is created in the student-teacher relationship which helps the teachers to be more empathetic towards students.

Table 5

Results of Two way ANOVA (2: Level of Education X 3: Level of Experience) and Tukey's HSD test for empathetic ability profile of women teachers

Source	SS	df	MS	F
Level of Education (A)	871.60	1	871.60	37.44**
Level of Experience (B)	5054.55	2	2527.28	108.56**
AXB	45.16	2	22.58	0.97
Error	9637.92	414	23.28	

Level of Education	Graduates & Post Graduates			Intermediates & Matriculates		
Level of Experience	<5 yrs.	15-20 yrs.	> 30 yrs.	<5 yrs.	15-20 yrs.	> 30 yrs.
Mean	14.32	18.19	20.21	14.54	16.71	18.45
	(1)	(2)	(3)	(4)	(5)	(6)
SD	4.46	4.83	5.61	5.49	4.58	5.06
Combined Mean (Edn.)	Graduates- 17.57			Intermediates-16.57		
Combined Mean (Exp.)	<5 yrs.-14.43		15-20 yrs.-17.45		> 30 yrs.-19.33	
Significant mean differences inTukey's HSD Test:						
Level of Education	2vs.5; 3vs.6					
Level of Experience	1vs.2;1vs.3; 2 vs.3; 4vs.5; 4vs.6; 5vs.6					

Note:- * <.05; ** p<.01

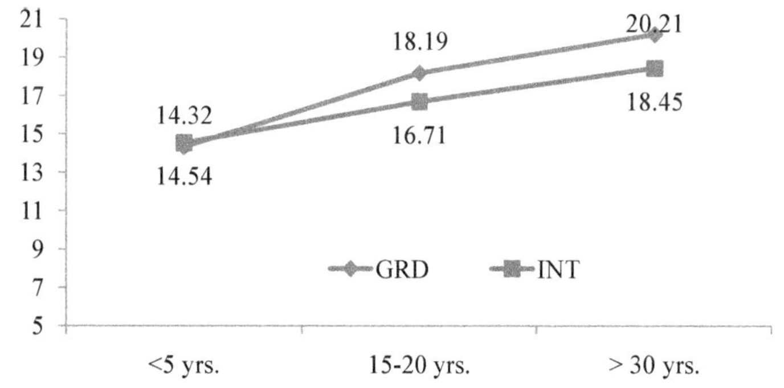

Figure 4a. Empathetic ability of women teachers compared for level of education

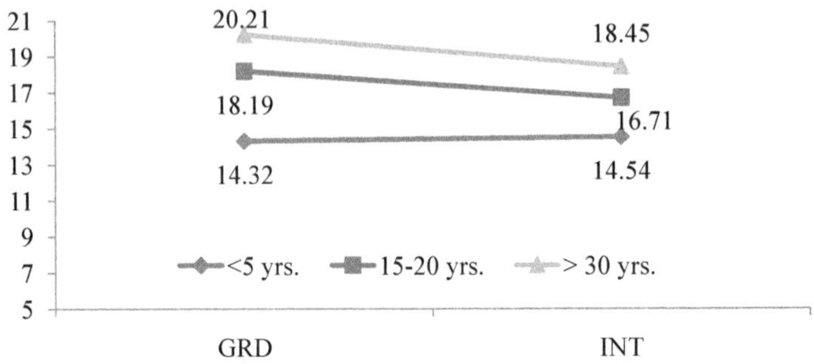

Figure 4b. Empathetic ability of women teachers compared for level of experience

Sensitivity profile. The teachers' sensitivity profile refers to his /her awareness about the socio-cultural needs of the students. Every class is a combination of students having varied socio-cultural needs. For example, students coming from different caste groups, socioeconomic groups and minority groups do not undergo similar socio-cultural needs and hence they require teachers' support for their needs which can be addressed by the sensitivity profile of the teachers. The results of ANOVA and Tukey's HSD test relating to the sensitivity profile of women primary teachers are reported in Table 6 and the corresponding group means are presented in Figure 5a and Figure 5b. It is observed in the results of ANOVA that the main effect of only the level of experience is significant [F (2, 414) = 67.58, p <.01] while the main effect of level of education [F (1, 414) = 2.26, p >.05] and the interaction effect [F (2, 414) = 1.95, p >.05] are not significant. On the other hand, Tukey's HSD test pointed out that for graduate and intermediate teachers, the sensitivity profile increases rapidly during the early years of experience in teaching and gradually it becomes slow in the later years. The findings may be supported from the fact that the sensitivity profile of the teachers is influenced by the socio-cultural experience of the teachers which naturally develop by their interaction with students from different socio-cultural groups. Several prior studies (Bloom, 2008; Gay, 2000; Gorton, 2003; Nieto, 2004) have reported that socio-culturally sensitive teachers create positive outcomes for all students and demonstrate better classroom management. In the paper, "Affirming diversity: The socio-political context of multicultural education", Nieto (2004) reported that multicultural sensitivity among the teachers is the most significant factor contributing to teacher effectiveness. Arising from the results of the present study, it may be suggested that there should fare distribution of experienced women teachers across the primary schools of Odisha because teacher's experience is a vital factor of his/her socio-cultural sensitivity.

Table 6

Results of Two way ANOVA (2: Level of Education X 3: Level of Experience) and Tukey's HSD test for sensitivity profile of women teachers

Source	SS	df	MS	F
Level of Education (A)	45.09	1	45.09	2.26
Level of Experience (B)	2696.44	2	1348.22	67.58**
AXB	77.82	2	38.91	1.95
Error	8259.30	414	19.95	

Level of Education	Graduates & Post Graduates			Intermediates & Matriculates		
Level of Experience	<5 yrs.	15-20 yrs.	> 30 yrs.	<5 yrs.	15-20 yrs.	> 30 yrs.
Mean	11.26	16.39	18.14	10.36	16.37	17.78
	(1)	(2)	(3)	(4)	(5)	(6)
SD	4.28	3.91	3.84	3.45	3.77	4.53
Combined Mean (Edn.)	Graduates- 15.26			Intermediates-14.83		
Combined Mean (Exp.)	<5 yrs.-10.81		15-20 yrs.-16.38		> 30 yrs.-17.76	
Significant mean differences inTukey's HSD Test:						
Level of Education	Nil					
Level of Experience	1vs.2;1vs.3; 2 vs.3; 4vs.5; 4vs.6; 5vs.6					

Note:- * <.05; ** p<.01

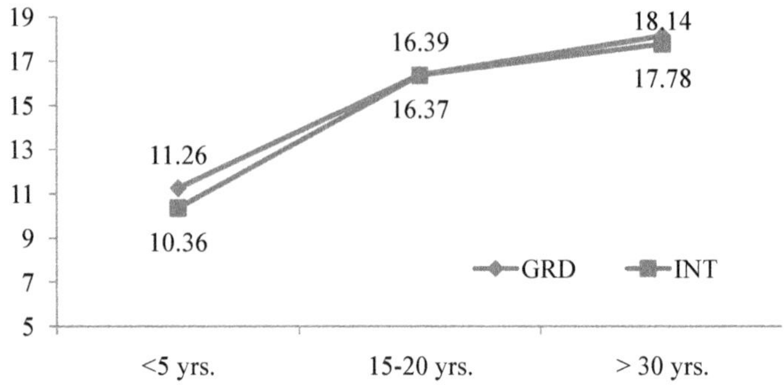

Figure 5a. Sensitivity profile of women teachers compared for level of education

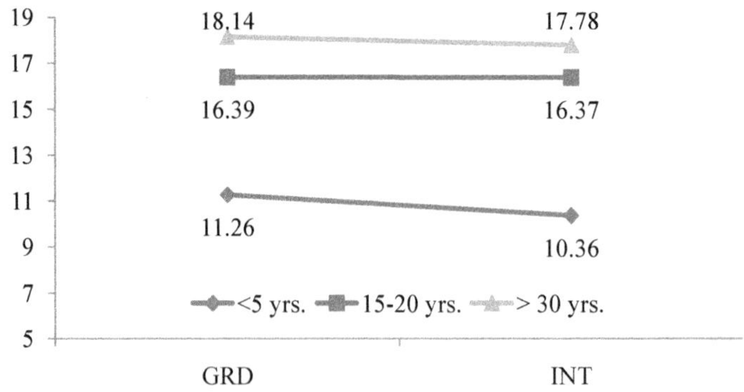

Figure 5b. Sensitivity profile of women teachers compared for level of experience

Sense of humor. Although many of us have a general sense of what it means to learn, there are often many assumptions involved. Teachers often assume that because they are "teaching", students must be learning. Students assume that because they have read their text and memorized facts, they have learned (Bacay, 2006). However, several evidences indicate that teachers' sense of humor is related positively to increasing learners' intrinsic motivation which results in better academic achievements (Lovern, 2008). Unfortunately, students often consider many of their classes boring, difficult and stressful. Torok et al., (2004) reported that sense of humor is one instructional tool that teachers can use in the classroom to overcome these feelings among the students and increase their effectiveness as teachers. Hence, teachers need to be trained in the use of humor as a part of any curriculum. The results of ANOVA relating to teachers' sense of humor are presented in the Table 7. Again it is found that the main effect of level of experience is only significant [$F (2, 414) = 85.33$, $p <.01$], while the main effect of level of education [$F (1, 414) = 3.07$, $p <.01$] and the interaction effect [$F (2, 414) = 1.66$, $p >.05$] are not significant. The results of Tukey's HSD test and Figures 6a and 6b have also clearly shown that teachers' sense of humor increases consistently with their increasing experience in teaching. Arising from the findings of the present study, it may also be suggested that training and counseling programs should be developed to improve the teachers' sense of humor and experienced teachers should interact with young teachers to help them improve their sense of humor in teaching.

Table 7

Results of Two way ANOVA (2: Level of Education X 3: Level of Experience) and Tukey's HSD test for sense of humor of women teachers

Source	SS	df	MS	F	
Level of Education (A)	64.47	1	64.47	3.07	
Level of Experience (B)	3583.86	2	1791.93	85.33**	
AXB	69.65	2	34.82	1.66	
Error	8694.00	414	21.00		
Level of Education	Graduates & Post Graduates			Intermediates & Matriculates	
Level of Experience	<5 yrs.	15-20 yrs.	> 30 yrs.	<5 yrs.	15-20 yrs.	> 30 yrs.
Mean	10.36	14.19	15.17	10.87	13.93	15.87
	(1)	(2)	(3)	(4)	(5)	(6)
SD	4.06	3.94	3.81	3.25	3.85	3.56
Combined Mean (Edn.)	Graduates- 13.24			Intermediates-13.55		
Combined Mean (Exp.)	<5 yrs.-10.62		15-20 yrs.-14.06		> 30 yrs.-15.52	
Significant mean differences inTukey's HSD Test:						
Level of Education	Nil					
Level of Experience	1vs.2;1vs.3; 2 vs.3; 4vs.5; 4vs.6; 5vs.6					

Note:- * <.05; ** p<.01

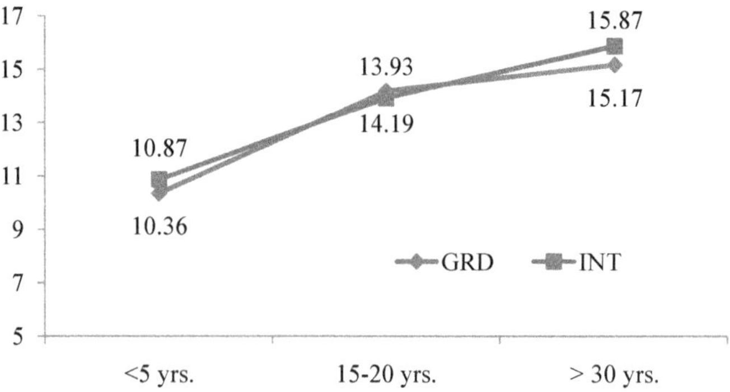

Figure 6a. Sense of humor of women teachers compared for level of education

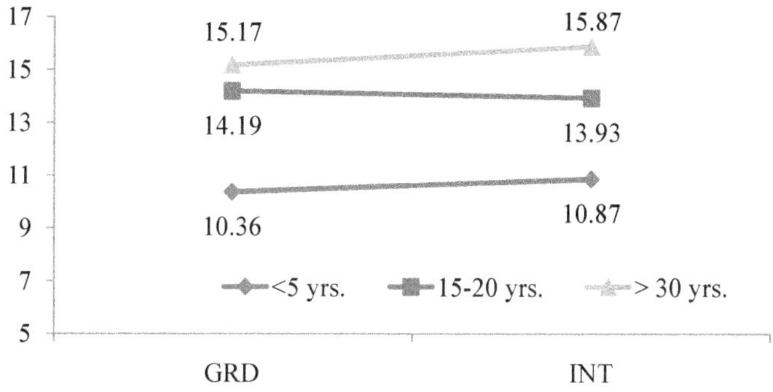

Figure 6b. Sense of humor of women teachers compared for level of experience

Punishing behavior. Teachers punishing behavior has been a controversial issue in the research literature. While most of research findings suggest that teacher's punishing behavior is ultimately a handicap for the students, some of the research also point to punishment management as a teacher skill to induce discipline among the students. However, a large number of researches claim that punishing behavior of teachers for primary school children has negative impact on students' development. Shah (2012) reviewing on the impact of teachers' behavior on students' self regulation pointed out that there is a strong positive correlation between the teachers' friendly relationship and students' eagerness for discipline. There is a positive and significant relationship between teachers' amount of respect for students and students disciplined behavior. There is also a significant relationship between teachers' self-regulation model and students' acceptance of discipline and he categorically pointed out that punishment is no solution to students' problem. The results of ANOVA in the present study relating to teachers punishing behavior pointed out that the main effect of only level of experience is significant [F (2, 414) = 103.59, p <.01], while the main effect of level of education [F (2, 414) = 0.77, p >.05], and interaction effect [F (2, 414) = 1.13, p >.05] are not significant. It is also found in the results of Tukey's HSD test and the graphs presented in Figure 7a and 7b that there is a consistent decrease in the punishing behavior of teachers as they continue with their experience in teaching. Hence, it may be said that young teachers are more punishing than experienced teachers. Counseling and training programs should be extended to help the young teachers change their attitude toward punishing the students.

Table 8

Results of Two way ANOVA (2: Level of Education X 3: Level of Experience) and Tukey's HSD test for punishing behavior of women teachers

Source	SS		df	MS		F
Level of Education (A)	16.45		1	16.45		0.77
Level of Experience (B)	4425.36		2	2212.68		103.59**
AXB	48.27		2	24.14		1.13
Error	8843.04		414	21.36		
Level of Education	Graduates & Post Graduates			Intermediates & Matriculates		
Level of Experience	<5 yrs.	15-20 yrs.	> 30 yrs.	<5 yrs.	15-20 yrs.	> 30 yrs.
Mean	17.22	12.56	10.31	16.98	12.43	10.51
	(1)	(2)	(3)	(4)	(5)	(6)
SD	3.44	4.29	3.16	3.57	3.46	2.87
Combined Mean (Edn.)	Graduates- 13.36			Intermediates-13.31		
Combined Mean (Exp.)	<5 yrs.-17.10		15-20 yrs.-12.50		> 30 yrs.-10.41	
Significant mean differences inTukey's HSD Test:						
Level of Education	Nil					
Level of Experience	1vs.2;1vs.3; 2 vs.3; 4vs.5; 4vs.6; 5vs.6					

Note:- * <.05; ** p<.01

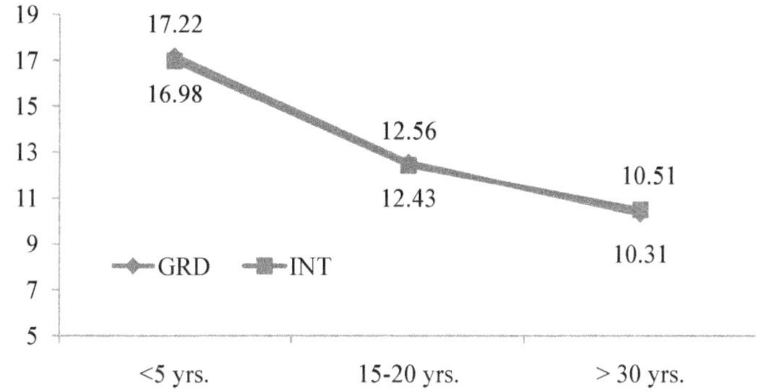

Figure 7a. Punishing behavior of women teachers compared for level of education

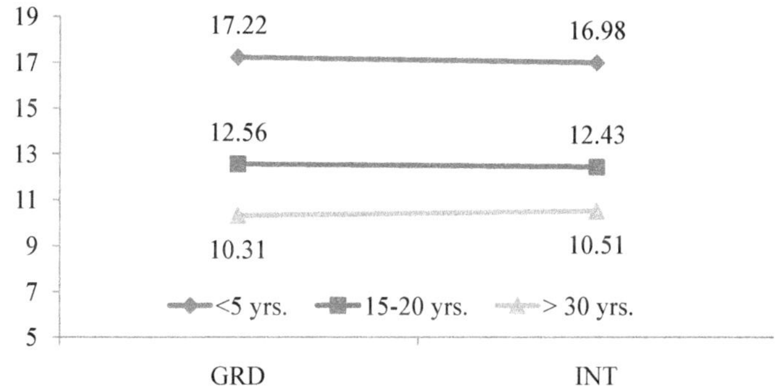

Figure 7b. Punishing behavior of women teachers compared for level of experience

Ethical and moral values. A study of Pantic and Wubbels (2012) examined the impact of teachers' ethical and moral value on their interpersonal relationship with students and arousal of cultural competence among the students. They observed that teachers' moral value has a strong impact on the affiliation and control of the students. They have also reported a positive association between teachers' moral values and students metacognitive and motivational components of cultural competence. In the results of ANOVA, it is also found that the main effect of only the level of experience of teachers' ethical and moral values is significant [$F (2, 414) = 152.77$, $p <.01$], while the main effect of level of education [$F (1, 414) = 1.91$, $p >.05$], and also the effect of interaction are not significant [$F (2, 414) = 2.15$, $p >.05$]. From the results of Tukey's HSD test it is also found that the teachers' ethical and moral values consistently increase with their experience in teaching. Figure 8a and 8b also point to the fact that level of education is not a factor of teachers' ethical and moral values, rather their experiences help them to grow in this skill.

Table 9

Results of Two way ANOVA (2: Level of Education X 3: Level of Experience) and Tukey's HSD test for ethical / moral values of women teachers

Source	SS	df	MS	F
Level of Education (A)	30.21	1	30.21	1.91
Level of Experience (B)	4833.64	2	2416.82	152.77**
AXB	68.01	2	34.00	2.15
Error	6549.48	414	15.82	

Level of Education	Graduates & Post Graduates			Intermediates & Matriculates		
Level of Experience	<5 yrs.	15-20 yrs.	> 30 yrs.	<5 yrs.	15-20 yrs.	> 30 yrs.
Mean	12.24	15.68	19.45	12.44	16.07	18.93
	(1)	(2)	(3)	(4)	(5)	(6)
SD	2.45	3.08	3.19	2.73	2.54	3.17

Combined Mean (Edn.)	Graduates- 15.79	Intermediates-15.81	
Combined Mean (Exp.)	<5 yrs.-12.34	15-20 yrs.-15.88	> 30 yrs.-19.19

Significant mean differences inTukey's HSD Test:

Level of Education	Nil
Level of Experience	1vs.2;1vs.3; 2 vs.3; 4vs.5; 4vs.6; 5vs.6

Note:- * <.05; ** p<.01

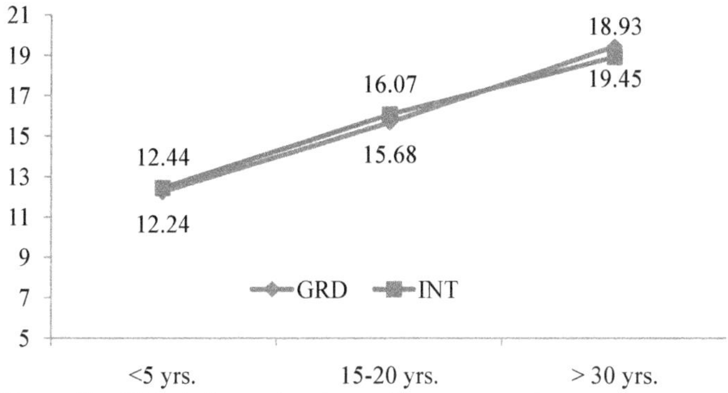

Figure 8a. Ethical / moral values of women teachers compared for level of education

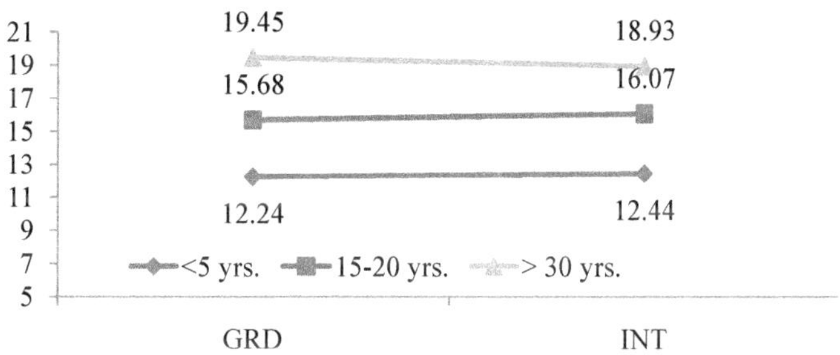

Figure 8b. Ethical / moral values of women teachers compared for level of experience

Superstition. Superstitious beliefs are irrational beliefs and notions held by human beings, which are based on fear, magical thinking, ignorance, and blind faith. These beliefs and notions do not have any basis in logic, facts, common sense, or in reality. Some of these beliefs include beliefs in God, ghost, charms, witches, black magic, miracles and black medicines. Olorundare (1998) reported from a study on Nigerian students that superstitious beliefs of teachers have a negative effect on students learning of science and tend to impede students' conceptualization of scientific knowledge by creating an existing prior knowledge which is in contrast with the scientific knowledge to be learned. Albert (2010) in a study of relationship between scientific literacy and African teachers' superstitious beliefs pointed out that science and superstition are not compatible with teachers and superstitious teachers not only are poor science teachers, they do have also less impact on students' performance. Evidence also exist to suggest that African students do not utilize what they learn in science in real life (Shumba, 1999) because they go through the ordeal of memorizing what is necessary to pass in the examination after which they return to the security of their traditional beliefs. The international association for the evaluation of educational achievement (IEA) also pointed to the poor performance of students in science in developing countries when compared to their counterparts in the developed countries which they assigned to their superstitious traditional beliefs (Postlethwaite & Wiley, 2010).

In the present study, it is found that the main effect of both the level of education [$F(1, 414) = 1.58$, $p > .05$], and the level experience [$F(2, 414) = 2.39$, $p > .05$], are not significant. The interaction effect is not also significant [$F(2, 414) = 0.91$, $p > .05$]. Hence, it may be concluded that superstition is a deep rooted cultural attribute of a teacher which cannot be easily changed and therefore, specific counseling and training programs should be developed to address this limitation among the teachers so that students get better quality education not only in science but in other fields also.

Table 10

Results of Two way ANOVA (2: Level of Education X 3: Level of Experience) and Tukey's HSD test for superstition of women teachers

Source	SS	df	MS	F	
Level of Education (A)	14.89	1	14.89	1.58	
Level of Experience (B)	45.19	2	22.59	2.39	
AXB	17.23	2	8.62	0.91	
Error	3908.16	414	9.44		
Level of Education	Graduates & Post Graduates			Intermediates & Matriculates		
Level of Experience	<5 yrs.	15-20 yrs.	> 30 yrs.	<5 yrs.	15-20 yrs.	> 30 yrs.
Mean	11.37	11.29	12.22	12.13	11.77	11.24
	(1)	(2)	(3)	(4)	(5)	(6)
SD	1.57	1.91	2.43	1.28	2.10	2.26
Combined Mean (Edn.)	Graduates- 11.63			Intermediates-11.71		
Combined Mean (Exp.)	<5 yrs.-11.93		15-20 yrs.-11.53		> 30 yrs.-11.73	
Significant mean differences inTukey's HSD Test:						
Level of Education	Nil					
Level of Experience	Nil					

Note:- * <.05; ** p<.01

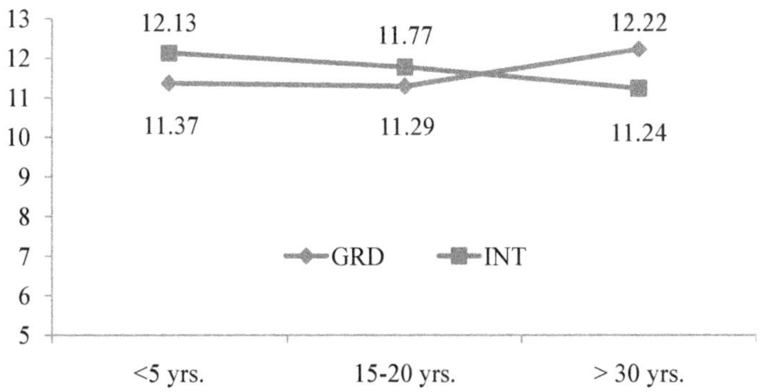

Figure 9a. Superstition of women teachers compared for level of education

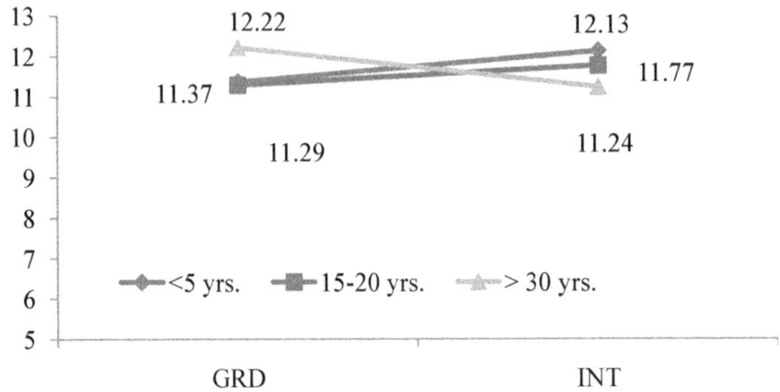

Figure 9b. Superstition of women teachers compared for level of experience

Flow mindset. There is increasing awareness among educators on the importance of fostering a flow mindset among the students and teachers. A recent survey by the Education Week Research Center (2016) indicated that 45 percent of teachers in USA were well acquainted with the concept of flow mindset, and almost all of them believe that nurturing a flow mindset in their students would improve their learning outcomes. Some teachers believe teaching is a natural ability that you either have or don't have (i.e., a fixed teaching mindset) whereas others believe teaching ability is something that can be developed (i.e., a growth teaching mindset). Just as with students, there are benefits of a flow mindset for the teachers. Gero (2013) reported from a study that teachers, who believe they can improve, seek out opportunities to learn, try to gather feedbacks for their teaching and appreciate appropriate constructive criticisms to improve their teaching while those with a fixed mindset are found as hesitant learners and take criticisms as a sign of their limited teaching ability. Auten (2013) reported from a study that teachers with flow mindset are not afraid to try new things in their classrooms and they continue to search out new pedagogical techniques in teaching. They encourage success in their students and help them perseverate in their study. These teachers are mostly appreciated by the students as effective teachers.

For the present study, it is found from the results of ANOVA that main effects of both level of education [F (1, 414) = 108.53, p <.01] and level of experience [F (2, 414) = 221.47, p <.01] are significant while the interaction effect is not significant [F (2, 414) = 2.96, p >.05]. It may be explained that teachers with higher level of education have undertook and practiced flow mindset because success in higher education demands more of flow mindset than fixed mindset. Reynolds (2006) reported from a study that less educated teachers see teaching in terms controlling: what students learn; how they learn, and how the learning is measured. On the other hand, teachers with higher education focused more on the learners and their learning processes rather than on teaching. Such findings clearly supported the results of the present study that teacher with higher education better nurture the flow mindset among the students than less educated teachers. Similar with other measures, the level of experience of teachers is also found to have strongly influenced their flow mindset. It may be explained that more experienced teachers gradually acquire more knowledge about student characteristics and their learning processes which help them develop a flow mindset in teaching.

Table 11

Results of Two way ANOVA (2: Level of Education X 3: Level of Experience) and Tukey's HSD test for flow mindset of women teachers

Source	SS	df	MS	F	
Level of Education (A)	805.29	1	805.29	108.53**	
Level of Experience (B)	3286.61	2	1643.31	221.47**	
AXB	43.93	2	21.96	2.96	
Error	3071.88	414	7.42		

Level of Education	Graduates & Post Graduates			Intermediates & Matriculates		
Level of Experience	<5 yrs.	15-20 yrs.	> 30 yrs.	<5 yrs.	15-20 yrs.	> 30 yrs.
Mean	10.26	16.18	20.33	8.66	11.23	14.16
	(1)	(2)	(3)	(4)	(5)	(6)
SD	1.27	2.04	3.16	1.35	2.32	2.85

Combined Mean (Edn.) Graduates- 15.59 Intermediates-11.35

Combined Mean (Exp.) <5 yrs.-9.46 15-20 yrs.-13.71 > 30 yrs.-17.25

Significant mean differences inTukey's HSD Test:

Level of Education 1vs. 4; 2vs.5; 3vs.6

Level of Experience 1vs.2;1vs.3; 2 vs.3; 4vs.5; 4vs.6; 5vs.6

Note:- * <.05; ** p<.01

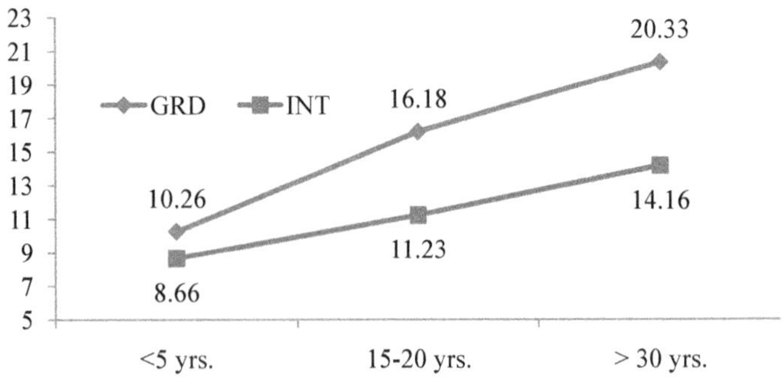

Figure 10a. Flow mindset of women teachers compared for level of education

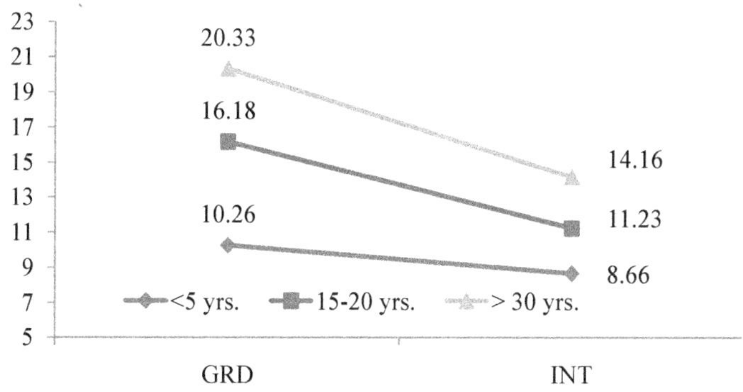

Figure 10b. Flow mindset of women teachers compared for level of experience

Summary of the findings. Level of education is found to have positively influenced only four of the ten attributes of teacher effectiveness. Those are self-image, locus of control, empathetic ability and flow mindset. But these are definitely very important and core attributes of an effective teachers. Hence, it is suggested that in the selection process of even primary teachers, higher academic qualification should have to be given due weightage so that more teachers with higher academic qualifications enter into the profession of teaching in the primary schools of Odisha. However, on the other hand, 9 of the 10 teacher effectiveness attributes excepting superstition are significantly influenced by the level of experience of the teachers. Hence, teacher experience is undoubtedly the best thing that the administration should think of when managing the affairs of teachers for primary education in Odisha. One of the suggestions may be that the distribution of teachers in the primary schools of Odisha should have a policy of fair distribution senior and junior teachers in each of the schools.

Psychological Capital of Women Primary Teachers in Odisha

Psychological capital is defined as the positive and developmental state of an individual characterized by high self-efficacy, optimism, hope and resiliency (Luthans & Youssef, 2004).They defined Self efficacy as people's confidence in their ability to achieve a specific goal in a specific situation. Hope is defined as a positive motivational state where two basic elements-successful feeling of agency or goal oriented determination and pathways or proactively planning to achieve those goals interact. Optimism is defined as a mental attitude of an individual as reflecting a belief that the outcome of some specific endeavor will be positive, favorable, and desirable. Finally, resilience is defined as a positive way of coping with adversity or distress. It is an ability to recover from stress, conflict, failure, change or increase in responsibility. Several studies have reported that psychological capitals are significant contributors to teachers' effectiveness. Rehman and Ali (2017) reported that psychological capital increases job satisfaction, commitment, and motivation for teaching among the teachers. Peterson et al., (2011) conducting a meta-analysis of 26 independent studies found strong, significant and positive relationships between teachers psychological capital and their desirable attitudes such as satisfaction, commitment, and wellbeing;

between teachers psychological capital and their performance as self-rated, supervisor rated and objective; and finally a negative relationship between teachers psychological capital and undesirable attitudes such as cynicism, stress and anxiety. Similarly, Luthans, Norman, Avolio and Avey (2008) reported that PsyCap develops a positive climate necessary for teachers' resources in order to achieve stable growth and teachers with strong PsyCap proved to be assets for their colleagues, students and schools. In view of such significance of psychological capital for teachers, the presented study has also measured all the four PsyCap of the women teachers and reported the means, standard deviations, combined means and combined standard deviations for each of these measures in Table 12.

(i) General assessment of the teacher's PsyCap. In order to correspond to other measures of the study, the maximum score for each attribute of the PsyCap and even of the total PsyCap are converted to a scale of 24. First of all, the combined means and combined standard deviations for all the six groups of subjects are used to find out an overall nature of the PsyCap among the women primary teachers in Odisha.

Out of a maximum score of 24, the average self-efficacy of the teachers is found to be 12.22 which are about a 51% skill. Hence, the self-efficacy of the women primary teachers in Odisha is not very good. The standard deviation of 2.81also points to the fact that many of the women primary teachers in Odisha are in a poor state of self-efficacy. Hence, it is desirable that this level of self-efficacy of the primary teachers' needs to be improved because many prior studies have reported that teacher's self-efficacy are foundation for students' success. Therefore, it is suggested that school administration should develop academic, training and counseling programs to help improve primary women teachers' self-efficacy.

Hope, as a PsyCap was also measured for the women teachers and the combined mean is found to be 11.80 with a standard deviation of 2.46. This PsyCap being only a 49% skill on the average is found to be low among the teachers. Some prior studies have reported that more than 65% of average skill in hope among the teachers is actually a good skill for the teacher effectiveness. Hence, it is obvious that the educational administration in Odisha needs to be concerned about enhancing the PsyCap of hope among the teachers to make the primary education more effective.

The average of optimism among the women teachers is still low as the combined mean is only 10.39 and in percentage term, it is only 43%. Hence, it should also be taken as a matter of concern to encourage more optimism among the women primary teachers so that the students get the benefit of their effectiveness as teachers. Resilience is found to be the best available PsyCap among the women primary teachers in Odisha. They are around 60% in this skill and standard deviation of only 2.58 point to the fact that many of the women teachers are strongly resilient which may also be due to the fact that socio-cultural contingencies have made them stronger and resilient as working women. Finally, the average of the total PsyCap is only 12.20 which is around 50% skill and not good enough for the teachers to very effective. It may be concluded that the women primary teachers in Odisha are not as good in their PsyCap as they are in their psychosocial attributes. Hence, an integrated approach needs to be developed for training and counseling of the primary teachers so that they grow up in their PsyCap abilities to be more effective teachers for students of primary education in Odisha.

Table 12
Means and Standard Deviations, combined means and combined standard deviations of Psychological Capital of Graduate and Intermediate Teachers for Three Levels of Teaching Experience

Education		Graduates & Post Graduates			Intermediates & Matriculates			Combined Mean & SD
Experience		<5 yrs.	15-20 yrs.	< 30 yrs.	<5 yrs.	15-20 yrs.	>30 yrs.	
self-efficacy (24)	Mean	8.64	12.91	16.12	8.55	12.41	14.69	12.22
	SD	3.26	2.27	2.32	3.15	2.61	2.54	2.81
Hope (24)	Mean	11.13	11.96	13.15	10.74	11.25	12.57	11.80
	SD	2.31	2.55	2.43	2.76	2.39	2.05	2.46
Optimism (24)	Mean	8.67	9.46	12.34	8.89	11.37	11.59	10.39
	SD	2.35	3.07	2.81	2.54	2.37	2.63	2.67
Resilience (24)	Mean	10.44	14.36	17.35	11.09	15.52	17.56	14.39
	SD	2.37	2.20	3.12	2.45	2.13	2.84	2.58
Total (24)	Mean	9.72	12.17	14.74	9.82	12.64	14.10	12.20
	SD	2.37	2.56	2.78	2.69	2.59	2.44	2.63

(ii) Group difference in psychological capital. In the present study, level of education and level of experience are used as independent factors to study group differences in the PsyCap of the women primary teachers. The results of the ANOVA and Tukey's HSD test for Self-efficacy are reported in Table 13 and graphs representing the corresponding means are presented in Figure 11a and 11b. It is observed that the main effects of both level of education [F (1, 414) = 8.96, p <.01] and level of experience [F (2, 414) = 73.41, p <.01] are significant while the interaction effect is not significant. It may be derived from the results that self-efficacy of teachers increases with both their level of education and level of experience. But the post-hoc comparisons point to the fact that teachers with higher education are significantly different in self-efficacy only among the most experienced group of teachers while at the lower level of experience differences were not found between teachers with higher and lower education. On the other hand, they are significantly better in self-efficacy at each level of increase in their experience. Sizes of the F-values are also clearly indicative of the fact that experience is a more desirable factor to increase the self-efficacy of the teachers than education. Hence, it may be suggested for reference of the administration that more teachers with higher education should be employed for teaching in primary classes and more importantly, there should be a fair distribution of experienced teachers in different primary schools of Odisha.

Table 13

Results of Two way ANOVA (2: Level of Education X 3: Level of Experience) and Tukey's HSD test for Self-efficacy (PsyCap)of women teachers

Source	SS	df	MS	F	
Level of Education (A)	59.76	1	59.76	8.96**	
Level of Experience (B)	979.29	2	489.64	73.41**	
AXB	28.68	2	14.34	2.15	
Error	2761.38	414	6.67		
Level of Education	Graduates & Post Graduates			Intermediates & Matriculates		
Level of Experience	<5 yrs.	15-20 yrs.	> 30 yrs.	<5 yrs.	15-20 yrs.	> 30 yrs.
Mean	8.64	12.91	16.12	8.55	12.41	14.69
	(1)	(2)	(3)	(4)	(5)	(6)
SD	3.26	2.27	2.32	3.15	2.61	2.54
Combined Mean (Edn.)	Graduates- 12.56			Intermediates-11.88		
Combined Mean (Exp.)	<5 yrs.-8.60		15-20 yrs.-12.66		> 30 yrs.-15.40	
Significant mean differences inTukey's HSD Test:						
Level of Education	3vs.6					
Level of Experience	1vs.2;1vs.3; 2 vs.3; 4vs.5; 4vs.6; 5vs.6					

Note:- * <.05; ** p<.01

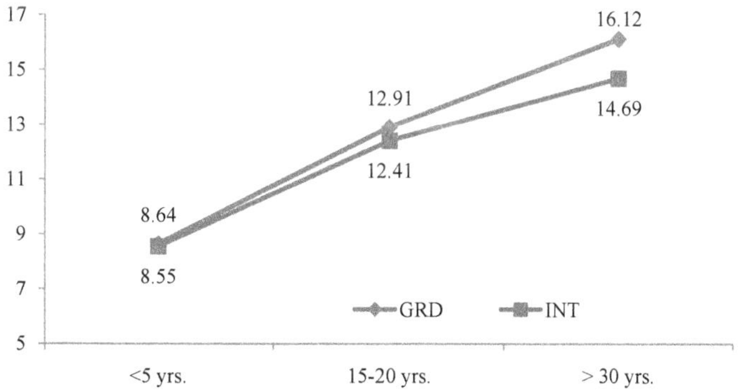

Figure 11a. Self-efficacy (PsyCap) of women teachers compared for level of education

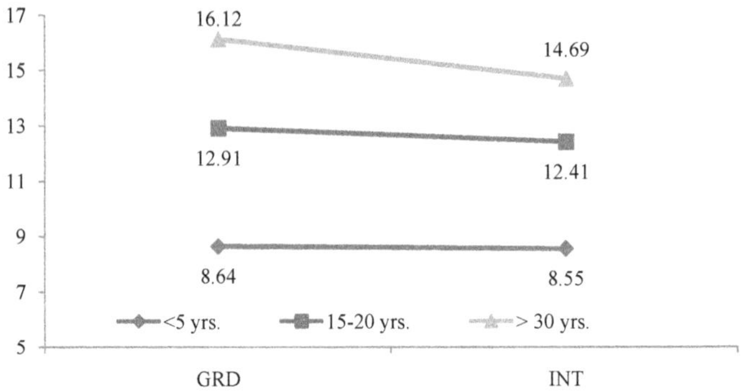

Figure 11b. Self-efficacy (PsyCap) of women teachers compared for level of experience

The results of ANOVA relating to group difference in hope are presented in Table 14 and the graphs relating to the group means are presented in Figures 12a and 12b. In the results of ANOVA, it is also found that the main effects of both level of education [F (1, 414) = 13.52, p <.01] and experience [F (2, 414) = 38.68, p <.01] are significant while the interaction effect is not significant. The results are very similar to that of the self-efficacy that experience is a more desirable factor to increase hope among the teachers than their level of education. However, from the results of Tukey's HSD test, it is found that although at lower level of experience, higher education does not make a difference in hope among the teachers, by 15 to 20 years of experience; education has a significant impact on the characteristics of hope among the teachers. On the other hand, hope among the teachers is found to have been consistently increasing with the experience of teachers. Hence, it may be further suggested for reference of the administration that more teachers with higher education should be employed for teaching in primary classes and most importantly, there should be a fair distribution of experienced teachers in different primary schools of Odisha.

Table 14

Results of Two way ANOVA (2: Level of Education X 3: Level of Experience) and Tukey's HSD test for Hope (PsyCap) of women teachers

Source	SS		df		MS	F
Level of Education (A)	97.75		1		97.75	13.52**
Level of Experience (B)	559.31		2		279.66	38.68**
AXB	33.84		2		16.92	2.34
Error	2993.22		414		7.23	
Level of Education	Graduates & Post Graduates			Intermediates & Matriculates		
Level of Experience	<5 yrs.	15-20 yrs.	> 30 yrs.	<5 yrs.	15-20 yrs.	> 30 yrs.
Mean	11.13	11.96	13.15	10.74	11.25	12.57
	(1)	(2)	(3)	(4)	(5)	(6)
SD	2.31	2.55	2.43	2.76	2.39	2.05
Combined Mean (Edn.)	Graduates- 12.08			Intermediates-11.52		
Combined Mean (Exp.)	<5 yrs.-10.94		15-20 yrs.-11.61		> 30 yrs.-12.86	
Significant mean differences inTukey's HSD Test:						
Level of Education	2 vs.5, 3vs.6					
Level of Experience	1vs.3; 2 vs.3; 4vs.6; 5vs.6					

Note:- * <.05; ** p<.01

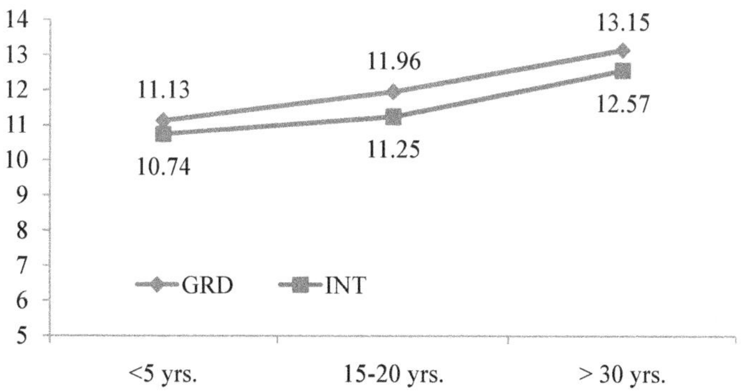

Figure 12a. Hope (PsyCap) of women teachers compared for level of Education

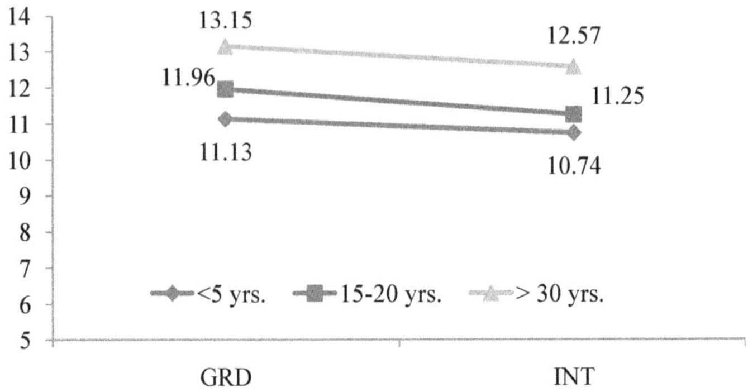

Figure 12b. Hope (PsyCap) of women teachers compared for level of Experience

The results of ANOVA and Tukey's HSD test for the PsyCap of Optimism are presented in Table 15 and the corresponding means are presented in Figure 13a and 13b. The results pointed out that the main effects of both level of education [F (1, 414) = 11.58, p <.01] and level of experience [F (2, 414) = 29.44, p <.01] are significant while the interaction effect is not significant. However, the results show some typical trend that intermediate teachers grow up in optimism during their initial service period and then continued in the same level while graduate teachers become more optimistic during the later phase of their service. Even graduate teachers are less in optimism compared to their counterparts among intermediate teacher during the middle period of their service. Although adequate explanation cannot be provided for such discrepancies, it may be assumed that better promotional prospects and higher responsibilities on senior graduate teachers are sources for differences in their optimism during their later service period. On the other hand, the fact remains that experience is a strong factor contributing to the development of optimism among both graduate and intermediate teachers. Therefore, administration should take note of this fact and make balanced distribution of experienced teachers in different primary schools of Odisha.

Table 15

Results of Two way ANOVA (2: Level of Education X 3: Level of Experience) and Tukey's HSD test for Optimism (PsyCap) of women teachers

Source	SS		df		MS	F
Level of Education (A)	152.39		1		76.20	11.58**
Level of Experience (B)	387.43		2		193.72	29.44**
AXB	20.13		2		10.07	1.53
Error	2724.12		414		6.58	
Level of Education	Graduates & Post Graduates			Intermediates & Matriculates		
Level of Experience	<5 yrs.	15-20 yrs.	> 30 yrs.	<5 yrs.	15-20 yrs.	> 30 yrs.
Mean	8.67	9.46	12.34	8.89	11.37	11.59
	(1)	(2)	(3)	(4)	(5)	(6)
SD	2.35	3.07	2.81	2.54	2.37	2.63
Combined Mean (Edn.)	Graduates- 10.16			Intermediates-10.62		
Combined Mean (Exp.)	<5 yrs.-8.78		15-20 yrs.-10.42		> 30 yrs.-11.96	
Significant mean differences inTukey's HSD Test:						
Level of Education	2 vs.5					
Level of Experience	1 vs.2; 1vs.3; 2 vs.3; 4vs.6					

Note:- * <.05; ** p<.01

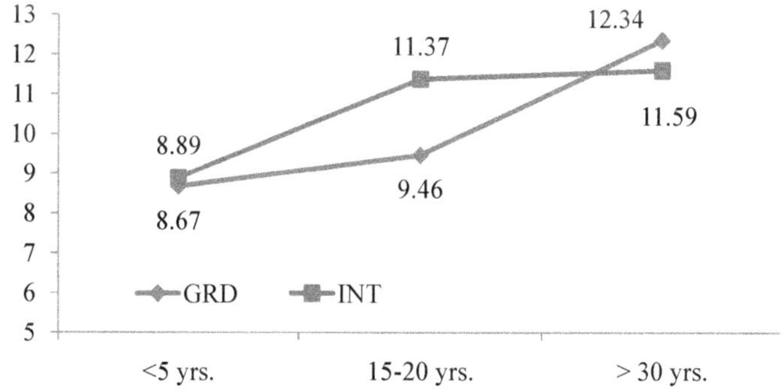

Figure 13a. Optimism (PsyCap) of women teachers compared for level of Education

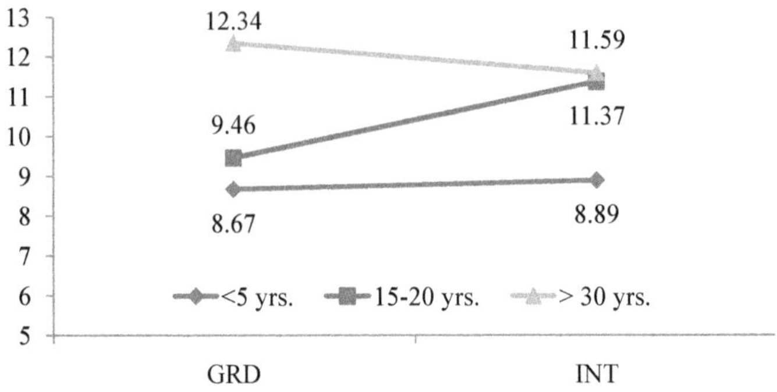

Figure 13b. Optimism (PsyCap) of women teachers compared for level of Experience

The results of ANOVA and Tukey's test for the resilience of teachers in different groups are presented in Table 16 and graphs relating to the means are presented in Figure 14a and 14b. Although, the main effects of both level of education [$F(1, 414) = 8.67$, $p < .01$] and level of experience [$F(2, 414) = 107.53$, $p < .01$] are significant, the size of the F-value clearly pointed to the importance of experience in the development of resilience among the teachers. Post hoc tests also point out that all along the service career, both graduate and intermediate teachers grow up in their resilience and intermediate teachers are found to be more resilient than graduate teachers. Such findings may be attributed to their service conditions.

Table 16

Results of Two way ANOVA (2: Level of Education X 3: Level of Experience) and Tukey's HSD test for Resilience (PsyCap) of women teachers

Source	SS		df	MS		F
Level of Education (A)	150.00		1	75.00		8.67**
Level of Experience (B)	1903.28		2	951.64		107.53**
AXB	34.87		2	17.43		1.97
Error	3663.90		414	8.85		
Level of Education	Graduates & Post Graduates			Intermediates & Matriculates		
Level of Experience	<5 yrs.	15-20 yrs.	> 30 yrs.	<5 yrs.	15-20 yrs.	> 30 yrs.
Mean	10.44	14.36	17.35	11.09	15.52	17.56
	(1)	(2)	(3)	(4)	(5)	(6)
SD	2.37	2.20	3.12	2.45	3.13	2.84
Combined Mean (Edn.)	Graduates- 14.05			Intermediates-14.72		
Combined Mean (Exp.)	<5 yrs.-10.77		15-20 yrs.-14.94		> 30 yrs.-17.46	
Significant mean differences inTukey's HSD Test:						
Level of Education	2 vs.5					
Level of Experience	1 vs.2; 1vs.3; 2 vs.3; 4 vs.5; 5vs.6; 4vs.6					

Note:- * <.05; ** p<.01

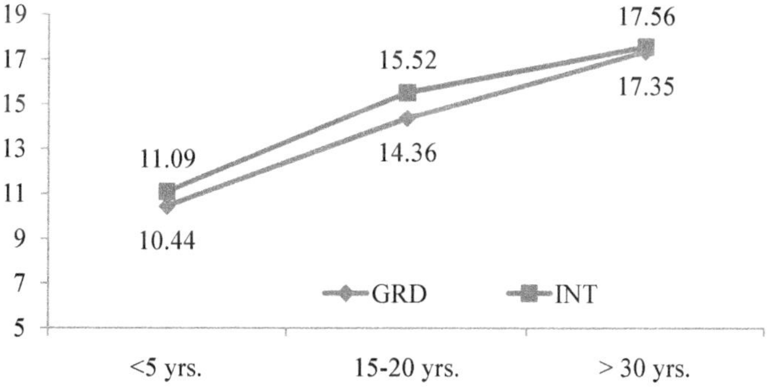

Figure 14a. Resilience (PsyCap) of women teachers compared for level of Education

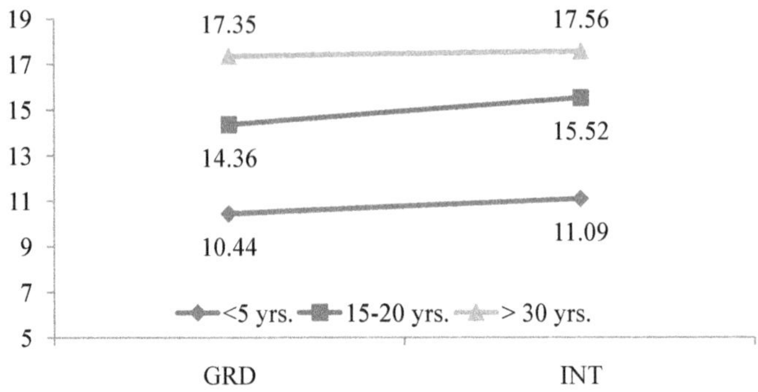

Figure 14b. Resilience (PsyCap) of women teachers compared for level of Experience

Summary of the findings. Arising from the results of the study on the PsyCap of the women primary teachers, it may be pointed out that although level of education of the teachers has some impact on the development of PsyCap among teachers, the impact is not as strong as it is from the experience of the teachers. In other words, the experience of the teachers is a very strong factor in the development of PsyCap of the teachers. Psychosocial attributes of teachers were also found to have been very strongly influenced by their experience. Hence, it may be concluded from the results of the present study that experience of teachers is the golden route to teachers' development of appropriate psychosocial attribute and psychological capital to help them to become more effective teachers. Therefore, training and counseling programs should be developed to help the primary teachers to have variety of exposure and experience relating to primary school children curriculum which will ultimately increase teacher effectiveness in all fronts of the students' life and success.

Teacher Effectiveness of Women Primary Teachers in Odisha

In the previous section discussions were presented about the psychosocial attributes and psychological capital of women primary teachers in Odisha. The next important evaluation is about their teacher effectiveness. Walker (2008) identified 10 measureable characteristics of teacher effectiveness from a 15-year of longitudinal study. He had engaged college students in discussions and writing assignments that pertain to the outstanding characteristics of their most effective teachers. Walker's identified characteristics of the effective teachers were: (i) come to class prepared, (ii) maintain positive attitudes about teaching and about students, (iii) hold high expectations for all students, (iv) show creativity in teaching the class, (v) treat and grade students fairly, (vi) display a personal and approachable touch with students, (vii) cultivate a sense of belongingness in the classroom, (viii) respect students and do not deliberately embarrass them, (ix) forgive students and do not hold grudges, and finally (x) admit their own mistakes. Walker has also developed a scale to measure teacher effectiveness. The effectiveness of each teacher in the present study was measured by a short scale of 60 items, 6 items measuring each of the 10 teacher effectiveness characteristics. The teachers were asked to evaluate them on a five-point scale (0-4) on each of the Walker's characteristics of teacher effectiveness and the total score obtained by a teacher on a construct is her score on the construct. Hence, on each of the characteristics, a teacher is evaluated on a scale of 24. The means, standard deviations for each subgroup of teachers, and their combined means and standard deviations for each of the characteristics of teacher effectiveness are presented in Table 17.

(i) General assessment of Teacher Effectiveness

Preparedness. According to Walker the most effective teachers come to class each day ready to teach. It is easy to learn in their classes because they are ready for the day. They don't waste instructional time. They start class on time and teach the entire period. Time flies in their classes because students are engaged in learning. Patrick and Smart (1998) in a study on empirical evaluation of teacher effectiveness found three critical factors of teaching namely; respect for students, ability to challenge students, and preparedness of the teacher in terms of organization and presentation skills. Newton et al., (2012) carried out a series of regression analyses on 4th and 5th grade students' achievement gains on six different reading and mathematics tests. He found that prepared teachers consistently produced stronger student achievement gains than unprepared teachers even controlling for teachers' experience, degrees, and student characteristics. Shamina and Muthas (2018) reported from a study that the preparedness of the teachers creates a positive classroom context for teachers and students resulting in higher exchange or communication among teachers and students, more positive feedbacks, and better appreciation of the teaching learning process. Many such studies in research literature have been found to advocate for preparedness as an important skill for teacher effectiveness.

In the present study, the combined mean of preparedness is 13.98 with a standard deviation of 2.17. Out of a maximum score of 24, the women primary teachers of Odisha are found to have 58.25% preparedness on the average. Although, it is a good standard on the average, the standard deviation of 2.17 points to the fact that many of the teachers actually go to the class less prepared. Hence, it is important that the school administration should take care to guide the teachers to come prepared to the class with appropriate lesson notes and lesson plans.

Positive Attitude. Walker reported that most effective teachers have optimistic attitude about teaching and about students. They make themselves available to all students. They communicate with students about their progress and give praise and recognition when required. They also use strategies to help students act positively towards one another. Ulug, Ozden, and Eryilmaz (2011) in a study on the effects of teachers' attitudes on students' personality and performance reported that teachers' positive attitudes have influenced both students' personality and academic performance. They have observed that in the class of the teachers with positive attitudes, the confidence level, intrinsic motivation, classroom and peer interaction, attendance in the class, and teacher-student communication inside and outside the class are significantly more than for the same students in the class of a teacher with negative attitudes. Several such studies in the literature provide evidence that teachers' positive attitude is great source of students' personality development and achievements in life. In the present study, with regard to the positive attitudes of women primary teachers, the combined mean is 13.00 with a standard deviation of 2.35. Similarly, out of a maximum score of 24, the teachers are only in the level of 54.16% in the skill. It is actually not a very good average relating teachers' positive attitude. Further, the standard deviation is also high enough to point out that many of the teachers have very low positive attitude towards the students and the teaching -learning process. Hence, school administration should be concerned about this fact and develop counseling programs for the teachers to help them grow positive attitudes towards students and teaching learning processes.

Hold high expectations. According to Walker, most effective teachers set no limit on students and believe everyone can be successful. They hold the highest standard of reference for their students; consistently challenge their students to do the best, and build students' confidence and teaching them to believe in themselves. The importance of teacher expectations in facilitating students' learning and performance has long been recognized (Rubie-Davies, 2008). On the basis of different reviews and meta-analyses, the average effect of teacher expectations on student performance has been found to be moderate to high (Jussim & Harber, 2005). Boer and Bosker (2010) reported from a study that negative teacher expectations have a detrimental influence on students' performance while positive expectations of the teachers have positive influence not only on the academic performance of the students but also on their future career. Weinstein, (2002) also observed from a study that younger children are more susceptible to teachers' expectations than older children. Hence, no doubt, teachers' positive expectation of students is a great source of teacher effectiveness. In the present study, the combined mean for positive teacher expectation of students is 12.86 and the combined standard deviation is 2.65. Out of a maximum score of 24, the teachers have 53.58% positive expectations on the average and definitely, this is not good standard with respect to teacher expectations. Further, a standard deviation of 2.65 also point to the fact that many of the teachers have very low expectations about their students which would have detrimental effects on the achievement motivation of the students. Hence, it is a matter of concern and school administration should prepare counseling programs for the teachers to help them understand their students and nurture strong positive expectations about them.

Creative. According to Walker effective teachers are resourceful and innovative in how they teach their classes. These creative teachers are prepared to take risk and remain open to new ideas. They are open-minded and use what's around them to help them create innovative ideas and teaching strategies for their classroom. In fact creative teachers promote more meaningful learning, student engagement, peer interaction, problem solving and reflective skills among the students. They also use the technology most effectively in the classroom. Manurung et al. (2017) observed in a study by analyzing the interview contents, teaching plans, teachers' reflections and classroom observations that creative teaching arouses strong curiosity, persistence, willingness to develop, acceptance of new experiences, self-confidence, depth of ideas, sense of humor, and imagination among students. Many such studies in the literature have pointed to the significance of creative teachers in giving out most effective teaching which has a lasting impact on the students' ability and performance. In the present study, the combined mean for creativity in teaching among the women primary school teachers in Odisha is only 10.87 and combined standard deviation is 2.96. Hence, out of a maximum of 24, the average is only 45.30% which is definitely a poor skill among the teachers. Hence, it is desirable that all teachers should develop the ability for creative teaching, which is essential in developing a flow mindset among the children. Therefore, it may be suggested that appropriate training programs should be prepared and women primary teachers should be exposed to creative teaching methods for different subjects that children study in primary classes.

Fair. According to Walker, effective teachers handle all students without discrimination and grade them appropriately. They allow all students equal opportunities and privileges; recognize that 'fair' does not necessarily mean treating everyone the same but means giving every student an opportunity to succeed, and understand that not all students learn in the same way and at the same rate. Although one might expect students to be most concerned with outcome or procedural fairness because it affects their grades, Rodabaugh (2015) has found that students consider violations of interactional fairness to be the most severe. Interactional fairness refers to the nature of the interaction between teacher and students which encompasses impartiality, respect, concern for students, and integrity of the teacher. Students expect the teacher to treat everyone in the class equally. Even subtle differences in how students are treated may lead to perceptions of partiality. The teacher who carefully monitors his behavior and avoids giving the impression of partiality becomes an effective teacher. Several other studies have also emphasized the significance of the fairness of the teachers in helping them to be effective teachers. In the present study, the combined mean with respect to the fairness of the women primary teachers in Odisha is 13.40 with a combined standard deviation of 2.74. It is only 55.83% of the maximum score which indicate that the women primary teachers are not very good in perception of fairness by their students. It is actually observed that in most of the cases, it results from some unintended behavior of the teachers. Hence, it is required that the teachers should be made aware of such behavior and undertake counseling practices to develop the skill of fairness behavior.

Personal concern. According to Walker, the most effective teachers are approachable and they connect with students personally. These teachers share personal experiences in the classes, take personal interest in students and find out as much as possible about them, and even play with them outside the normal school hours. Wentzel (1998) from her study on sixth grade students reported that supportive teacher-student relationships improved students' motivation at school, school and class related interests, academic goal orientations as well as pursuits on social goals. Muller (2001) reported from a study that positive teacher-student relationship is an important source of social capital for the students. Dika & Singh (2002) reported that social capital from positive teacher-student relationships can manifest itself in many different ways. For high school students, positive teacher-student relationships can reduce rates of dropping out by nearly half, help explore options for college, and provide support for further academic or vocational aspirations. Teacher-student relationships can have a significant effect on the peer acceptance of students. Teachers' interactions with students can affect classmates' perceptions of individual students, in turn affecting which students classmates choose to interact with and accept (Hughes et al., 2001). Many such studies in the research literature have shown that personal concern of the teacher is a significant source of teacher effectiveness.

In the present study, the combined mean of personal concern of women primary teachers in Odisha is 15.27 and the combined standard deviation is

2.66. The mean is actually 63.63% of the maximum score which is definitely a good average score in the skill. However, although many of the teachers are very good in the skill some of the teachers are not good as indicated by a high standard deviation. Hence, it may be suggested that counseling programs may used to help those teachers develop attitudes for developing positive relationships and personal concern with students.

Sense of belonging. According to Walker, the most effective teachers have a way of making students feel welcome and comfortable in their class. Students repeatedly mentioned that they felt as though they belonged in classrooms taught by effective teachers. The students knew they had a good teacher who loved teaching and preferred it to other occupations. A teacher's sense of belonging in school is the degree to which students feel respected, accepted and supported by the teacher. Kester (1994) reported from a study that teachers' sense of belonging to school are significantly linked to students' attention and effort in class, their persistence and completion of learning activities. He observed that improving teachers' sense of belonging to school also equally improves students' sense of belonging which help them to more actively engage in academic and non-academic activities, to put in more effort to become motivated in school activities. Juvonen (2006) even found that teachers' sense of belonging significantly reduced students' misbehavior, violence, dropout and even drug and alcohol abuse. Many such studies provided evidence that teachers' sense of belonging to school is very significant source of teacher effectiveness. In the present study, the combined mean for the women primary teachers' sense of belonging is 14.07 with a combined standard deviation of 2.75. Hence, this attitude of the women teachers is 58.62% on the average which in fact needs improvement. Further the standard deviation of 2.75 also point to the fact that many of the teachers are very low in the attitude. Therefore, it is suggested that measures need to be taken up by the school administration to help further improve the sense of belongingness to schools among the women primary teachers in Odisha.

Respect for students. According to Walker, the most effective teachers do not deliberately embarrass students. Teachers, who give the highest respect, get the highest respect. They respect students' privacy, speak to students in private concerning grades or conduct, show sensitivity to their feelings and consistently avoid situations that unnecessarily embarrass students. Meador (2018) reported from a regression analysis that respecting students is essential for boosting teacher effectiveness. Garza (2007) described teachers respect for students as providing the necessary scaffolds helping and expecting all students to reach their potential. Pang (2005) has reported that teachers' respect for students is a conscious and ethical responsibility that supports positive relationship building with the students. A significant body of research supports the importance of teachers' respect for students in the classroom. While student success and a teacher's ability to demonstrate genuine caring are linked, Collinson et al. (1998) acknowledged that caring teachers purposefully know their students well and establish relationships with them because students value the personal interaction. Many such studied in the literature have provided evidence that teachers' respect for students is a significant source of teacher effectiveness. In the present study, the combined mean of teachers' respect for students is 11.78 and the combined standard deviation is 2.51. As less than 50% of the maximum score, this attribute is, in fact, not good enough among the women primary teachers in Odisha. A standard deviation of 2.51 also point to the fact that many of the teachers are poor in this attribute. Hence, it may be suggested that teacher counseling programs should be arranged to help the teachers learn that respecting students is a major source of their effectiveness as teachers.

Forgiving. According to Walker the most effective teachers do not hold grudges. They forgive students for inappropriate behavior and understand that forgiving attitude is essential to reach to difficult students. They also understand that students' disruptive or antisocial behavior can quickly turn a teacher against a student, but a forgiving teacher is finally successful with difficult students. Forgiveness is accepted as one the universal human virtues and it is being discussed for its affective, cognitive, behavioral, moral and cultural consequences (Peterson & Seligman, 2004). Kerns (2009) reported from a study that teachers' forgiveness hinders destructive reactions among students and encourages constructive behavior among them. Hoy and Tarter (2011) in a study with college students reported that students' frustration and annoyance dissipates by teachers' forgiveness which otherwise become internalized into stress. He further reported that forgiveness is a powerful classroom management strategy because it encourages students to accept responsibility and accountability for their behavior while when teachers do not show forgiveness; students are encouraged to argue and point fingers to elsewhere. Many such studies have reported that the forgiving attitude of teachers is a highly significant source of teacher effectiveness. In the present study, the combined mean of forgiveness attitude among the women primary teachers of Odisha is 14.20 with a combined standard deviation of 2.58. These teachers having 60.83% of forgiving attitude clearly imply that they are very good in the skill. However, from a standard deviation of 2.58, it may be derived that there are also many teachers who are inadequate in the skill. Hence, it may be suggested to the administration that teacher counseling programs should be used to help the teachers understand the importance of forgiveness to student for better classroom management, better student-teacher relationship and more effectiveness in teaching.

Admitting mistakes. According to Walker, the most effective teachers are quick to admit being wrong. They apologize if mistakenly accused students. They also make corrections when students point out errors in scoring, grading or in test material. In fact limited studies have focused on how teachers deal with their mistakes in classroom settings. Tulis (2013) analyzed teachers' error management behavior based on data obtained from direct and videotaped systematic observations and students' reports. In the Study, associations between students' and teachers' attitudes towards mistakes and their impact on students' domain specific emotions were investigated. The findings also emphasize the relevance of how students perceive their teachers' attitudes towards mistakes. He observed that when teachers admit their mistakes, a safe and trusting learning environment is created in the class which influences the positive affective reactions of the students. For example, it increases enjoyment, satisfaction and pride among the students. Santagata (2005) has reported that teachers' admitting their mistakes, which he defined as a positive error climate in the classroom, improves students' motivation to achieve, their achievement, and their willingness to involve themselves in different tasks. On the other hand, when teachers do not admit their mistakes, what he called a negative error climate; it increases students' fear of failure, mal-adaptive motivational patterns and negative emotions. Hence, teachers' admitting their mistakes in the class is a significant source of teacher effectiveness. In the present study, the combined mean for women primary teachers admitting their mistakes in the classroom is 10.52, which is only 43.83% of the maximum score. A combined standard deviation of 2.37 also point to the fact that many of the teachers are not good in admitting their mistakes. Hence, it is suggested that proper counseling programs should be provided to the teachers to improve their attitude for admitting mistakes.

Table 17

Means and standard deviations, combined means and combined standard deviations of Teacher effectiveness of Graduate and Intermediate Teachers for Three Levels of Teaching Experience

Education		Graduates & Post Graduates			Intermediates & Matriculates			Combined Mean & SD
Experience		<5 yrs.	15-20 yrs.	< 30 yrs.	<5 yrs.	15-20 yrs.	>30 yrs.	
Prepared (24)	Mean	11.46	14.61	15.23	11.94	14.36	16.28	13.98
	SD	2.15	2.96	2.21	2.59	2.37	2.44	2.17
Positive (24)	Mean	10.35	12.96	15.84	10.87	13.45	14.51	13.00
	SD	2.24	2.56	3.11	3.07	2.63	2.84	2.35
Hold high expectations (24)	Mean	9.55	13.36	15.94	10.37	12.56	15.39	12.86
	SD	1.78	3.26	2.44	2.12	2.59	2.17	2.65
Creative (24)	Mean	7.61	12.94	17.36	5.38	9.44	12.45	10.87
	SD	2.07	3.14	2.93	1.76	2.68	2.57	2.96
Fair (24)	Mean	12.98	13.84	13.87	12.52	12.96	14.21	13.40
	SD	3.37	2.95	3.21	2.77	2.54	2.89	2.74
Personal Concern (24)	Mean	13.07	16.44	16.96	13.29	15.91	15.97	15.27
	SD	2.26	3.76	3.24	3.19	2.95	3.33	2.66
Sense of belonging (24)	Mean	12.17	15.63	15.91	11.96	13.39	15.37	14.07
	SD	2.07	2.11	2.89	2.54	2.15	2.06	2.75
Respect for students (24)	Mean	8.45	11.36	14.15	9.12	13.44	14.16	11.78
	SD	1.17	1.91	1.45	2.03	2.17	2.34	2.51
Forgiving (24)	Mean	12.65	15.11	16.23	11.96	14.57	14.69	14.60
	SD	3.17	2.39	2.34	2.56	2.36	2.67	2.58
Admitting mistakes (24)	Mean	7.39	10.65	13.12	8.36	10.67	12.94	10.52
	SD	2.45	2.39	2.51	2.07	2.66	2.54	2.37

Summary of the findings. It is observed in the results that while women primary teachers in Odisha are good in some of the teacher effectiveness skills like personal concern, sense of belonging, forgiving, and preparedness for the class, in some other skills like admitting mistakes, creativity, and respect for students, they are not good enough. Further, standard deviations in the range of 2.37 to 2.96 point to a good deal of diversity among the teachers with respect to the attributes of teacher effectiveness. Hence, it is suggested that an integrated program of awareness, counseling, and training should be developed to help those teachers to grow up in the desired skills.

Group Differences in Teacher Effectiveness Variables

The above discussions explained the state of affairs of the women primary teachers in Odisha with respect to different teacher effectiveness variables. Evidences from prior research point out that the teachers' education and experience are significant factors contributing to the effectiveness of teachers. As the present study is carried out on a 2 (level of education: intermediate and graduate) x 3 (experience: < 5years, 15-20 years, and > 30 years) factorial design, it is pertinent to examine group differences among the six subgroups so that more information would be available about the women primary teachers in Odisha. Results of two-way ANOVA including Tukey's HSD test for multiple comparison of means for each of the 10 teacher effectiveness variables are presented in Table 18 to Table 27.

The results of two-way ANOVA and Tukey's HSD test for the preparedness variable are reported in Table 18 and the graphs representing the group means are presented in Figures 15a and 15b. It is observed in the results that the main effect of both level of education [$F(1, 414) = 6.46$, $p < .05$] and level of experience [F (2, 414) = 71.44, p <.01] are significant, while the interaction effect is not significant. However, the results of HSD test point out that the intermediate teachers come more prepared to the class than the graduate teachers only during the later part of their service career. It may be due to the fact that most of the intermediate teachers were given to teach in the lower primary classes during their early service career, who were assigned to teach in higher primary classes as they become more experienced. Hence, because of their new and difficult assignments, they come more prepared to the classes. On the other hand, level of experience has a strong significant impact on the preparedness of the teachers. More experienced teachers come to the class better prepared.

Table 18

Results of Two way ANOVA (2: Level of Education X 3: Level of Experience) and Tukey's HSD test for Preparedness (TE) of women teachers

Source	SS	df	MS	F
Level of Education (A)	63.50	1	63.50	6.46*
Level of Experience (B)	1404.51	2	702.26	71.44**
AXB	44.24	2	22.12	2.25
Error	4069.62	414	9.83	

Level of Education	Graduates & Post Graduates			Intermediates & Matriculates		
Level of Experience	<5 yrs.	15-20 yrs.	> 30 yrs.	<5 yrs.	15-20 yrs.	> 30 yrs.
Mean	11.46	14.61	15.23	11.94	14.36	16.28
	(1)	(2)	(3)	(4)	(5)	(6)
SD	3.15	2.96	2.21	2.59	2.37	2.44

Combined Mean (Edn.)	Graduates- 13.77		Intermediates-14.19
Combined Mean (Exp.)	<5 yrs.-11.70	15-20 yrs.-14.49	> 30 yrs.-15.76
Significant mean differences inTukey's HSD Test:			
Level of Education	3 vs.6		
Level of Experience	1 vs.2; 1vs.3; 4 vs.5; 5vs.6; 4vs.6		

Note:- * <.05; ** p<.01

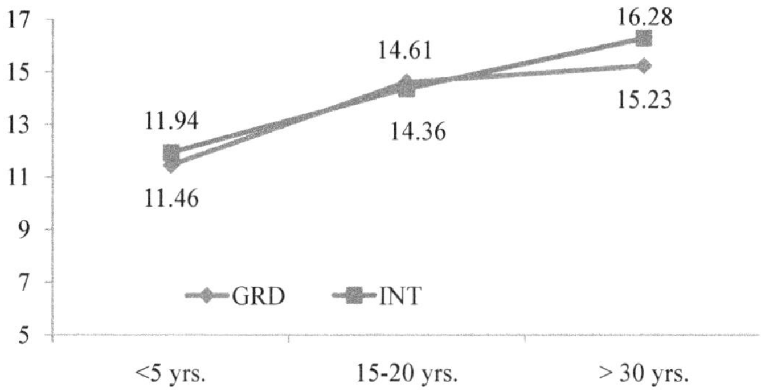

Figure 15a. Preparedness (TE) of women teachers compared for level of Education

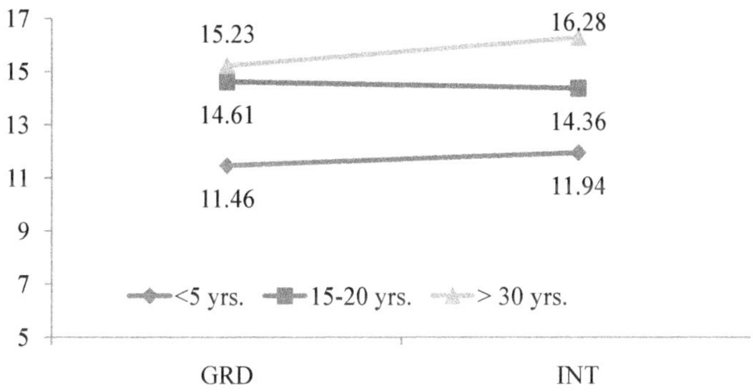

Figure 15b. Preparedness (TE) of women teachers compared for level of Experience

The results of two-way ANOVA and Tukey's HSD test for the variable of positive attitude are reported in Table 19 and the graphs representing the group means are presented in Figures 16a and 16b. It is observed in the results that the main effect of both level of education [F (1, 414) = 4.96, p <.05] and level of experience [F (2, 414) = 53.14, p <.01] are significant, and the interaction effect [F (2, 414) = 5.13, p <.05] is also significant. Results of

Tukey's test point out that the graduate and intermediate teachers only differ in their positive attitude during the later phase of their career which may be explained by the fact that graduate teachers get better service benefits than the intermediate teachers mostly during the later phase of service career for which they seem to have better job satisfaction and become more positive. On the other hand, level of experience has strong impact on the positive attitude of the teachers which should be due to growing awareness, expertise, and understanding of students.

Table 19

Results of Two way ANOVA (2: Level of Education X 3: Level of Experience) and Tukey's HSD test for Positive Attitude (TE) of women teachers

Source	SS		df		MS		F
Level of Education (A)	43.60		1		43.60		4.96*
Level of Experience (B)	934.20		2		467.10		53.14**
AXB	90.19		2		45.09		5.13*
Error	3639.06		414		8.79		
Level of Education	Graduates & Post Graduates			Intermediates & Matriculates			
Level of Experience	<5 yrs.	15-20 yrs.	> 30 yrs.	<5 yrs.	15-20 yrs.	> 30 yrs.	
Mean	10.35	12.96	15.84	10.87	13.45	14.51	
	(1)	(2)	(3)	(4)	(5)	(6)	
SD	2.24	2.56	3.11	3.07	2.63	2.84	
Combined Mean (Edn.)	Graduates- 13.05			Intermediates-12.94			
Combined Mean (Exp.)	<5 yrs.-10.61		15-20 yrs.-13.21		> 30 yrs.-15.18		
Significant mean differences inTukey's HSD Test:							
Level of Education	3 vs.6						
Level of Experience	1 vs.2; 1vs.3; 2 vs.3; 4 vs.5; 4vs.6						

Note:- * <.05; ** p<.01

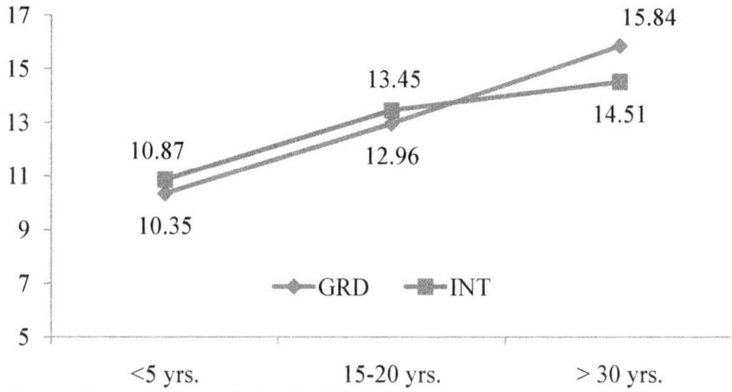

Figure 16a. Positive Attitude (TE) of women teachers compared for level of Education

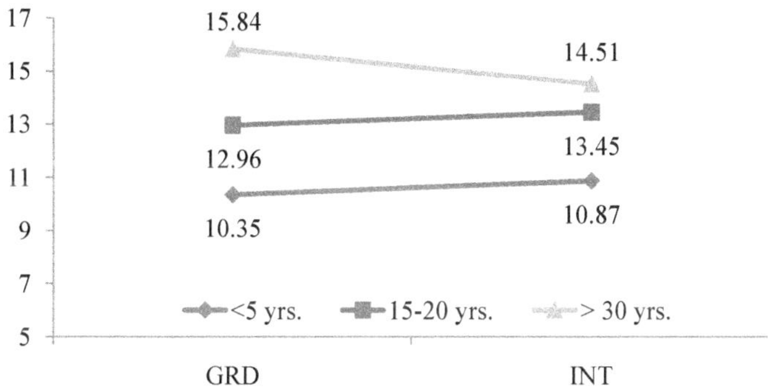

Figure 16b. Positive Attitude (TE) of women teachers compared for level of Experience

The results of two-way ANOVA and Tukey's HSD test for the variable of teacher expectation are reported in Table 20 and the graphs representing the group means are presented in Figures 17a and 17b. It is observed in the results that the main effect of only the level of experience [$F(2, 414) = 187.45$, $p < .01$] is significant, while the main effect of level of education and the interaction effect are not significant. Observed from the HSD results, it is found that teachers' high expectations of students consistently grow up as they become more and more experienced. It may be very clearly explained that growing with experience; teachers come to understand the students' perspective better and their expectations become more rational. Experienced teachers also understand the limitations of the students and help them overcome the limitations to fulfill their expectations about the students.

Table 20
Results of Two way ANOVA (2: Level of Education X 3: Level of Experience) and Tukey's HSD test for High Expectations (TE) of women teachers

Source	SS	df	MS	F
Level of Education (A)	18.88	1	18.88	3.39
Level of Experience (B)	2088.19	2	1044.10	187.45**
AXB	35.31	2	17.66	3.17
Error	2305.98	414	5.57	

Level of Education	Graduates & Post Graduates			Intermediates & Matriculates		
Level of Experience	<5 yrs.	15-20 yrs.	> 30 yrs.	<5 yrs.	15-20 yrs.	> 30 yrs.
Mean	9.55	13.36	15.94	10.37	12.56	15.39
	(1)	(2)	(3)	(4)	(5)	(6)
SD	1.78	3.26	3.44	2.12	2.59	3.17

Combined Mean (Edn.)	Graduates- 12.95		Intermediates-12.77
Combined Mean (Exp.)	<5 yrs.-9.96	15-20 yrs.-12.96	> 30 yrs.-15.67

Significant mean differences inTukey's HSD Test:

Level of Education	Not significant
Level of Experience	1 vs.2; 1vs.3; 2 vs.3; 4 vs.5; 4vs.6; 5vs.6

Note:- * <.05; ** p<.01

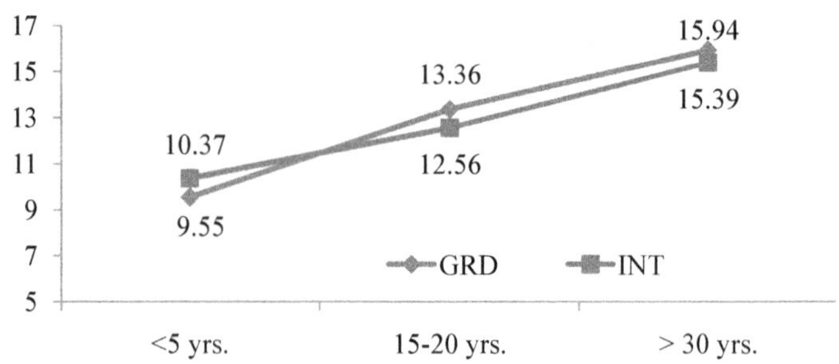

Figure 17a. High Expectations (TE) of women teachers compared for level of Education

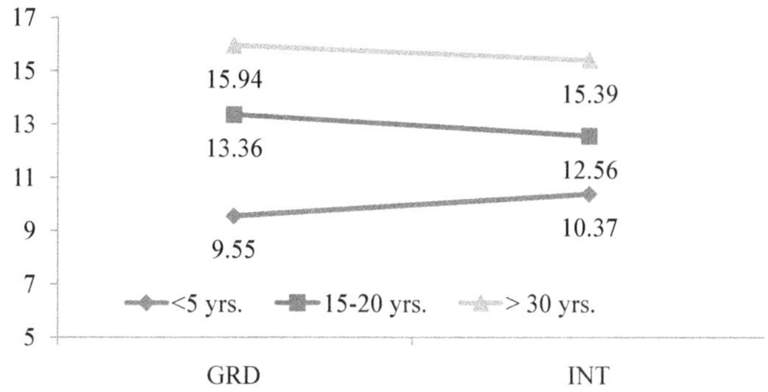

Figure 17b. High Expectations (TE) of women teachers compared for level of Experience

The results of two-way ANOVA and Tukey's HSD test for the variable of teacher's creativity are reported in Table 21 and the graphs representing the group means are presented in Figures 18a and 18b. It is observed in the results that the main effect of both level of education [$F(1, 414) = 33.88$, $p < .01$] and the level of experience [$F(2, 414) = 87.14$, $p < .01$], including the interaction effect [$F(2, 414) = 5.19$, $p < .05$] are significant. Results of multiple comparisons also point out that graduate teachers are consistently more creative than intermediate teacher which should be the impact of education and more exposure to higher and difficult curriculum which have made them more reflective and flexible in academics. On the other hand, experience has also consistently contributed to the development of creativity in teaching among both groups of teachers. Experiences no doubt make the teachers more flexible, reflective, diversified, risk-taking and challenging and therefore, they should be more creative in their teaching. The significant interaction effect may be explained by the fact that education provides the basis and experience provides the thrust to the teachers to become more creative in their teaching.

Table 21

Results of Two way ANOVA (2: Level of Education X 3: Level of Experience) and Tukey's HSD test for Creativity (TE) of women teachers

Source	SS	df	MS	F		
Level of Education (A)	210.73	1	210.73	33.88**		
Level of Experience (B)	1084.02	2	542.01	87.14**		
AXB	64.56	2	32.28	5.19*		
Error	2575.08	414	6.22			
Level of Education	Graduates & Post Graduates			Intermediates & Matriculates		
Level of Experience	<5 yrs.	15-20 yrs.	> 30 yrs.	<5 yrs.	15-20 yrs.	> 30 yrs.
Mean	7.61	12.94	17.36	5.38	9.44	12.45
	(1)	(2)	(3)	(4)	(5)	(6)
SD	2.07	3.14	2.93	1.76	2.68	2.57
Combined Mean (Edn.)	Graduates- 12.64			Intermediates-9.09		
Combined Mean (Exp.)	<5 yrs.-8.53		15-20 yrs.-11.19		> 30 yrs.-14.91	
Significant mean differences inTukey's HSD Test:						
Level of Education	1 vs.4; 2vs.5; 3vs.6					
Level of Experience	1 vs.2; 1vs.3; 2 vs.3; 4 vs.5; 4vs.6; 5vs.6					

Note:- * <.05; ** p<.01

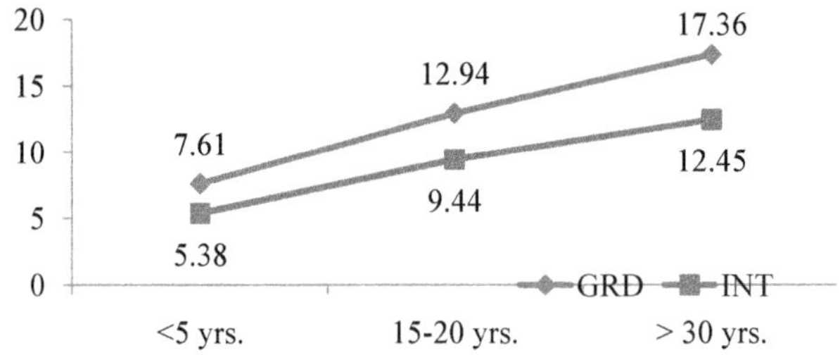

Figure 18a. Creativity (TE) of women teachers compared for level of Education

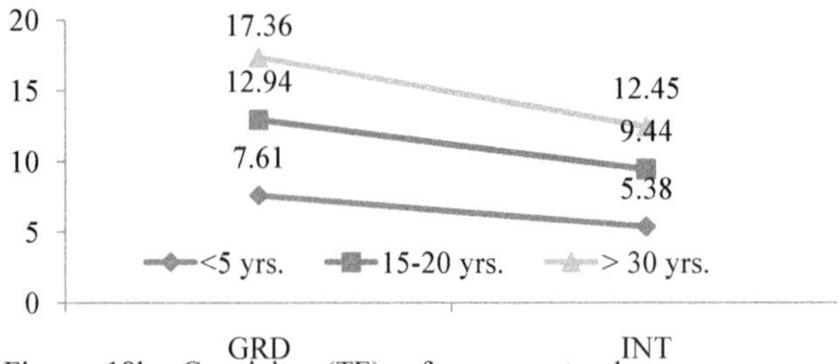

Figure 18b. Creativity (TE) of women teachers compared for level of Experience

The results of two-way ANOVA and Tukey's HSD test for the variable of teacher's fairness are reported in Table 22 and the graphs representing the group means are presented in Figures 19a and 19b. It is observed in the results that the main effect of only the level of experience [F (2, 414) = 27.55, p <.01] is significant and the main effect of level of education and the interaction effect are not significant. However, the results of Tukey's test only point out that the fairness among teachers develop strongly only during the later part of their service for both intermediate and graduate teachers. Hence, it may be said that experienced teachers become more stable in their thinking and attitude to be fair with all students.

Table 22

Results of Two way ANOVA (2: Level of Education X 3: Level of Experience) and Tukey's HSD test for Fairness (TE) of women teachers

Source	SS		df	MS		F
Level of Education (A)	39.77		1	39.77		3.71
Level of Experience (B)	590.62		2	295.34		27.55**
AXB	89.83		2	44.92		2.29
Error	4438.08		414	10.72		
Level of Education	Graduates & Post Graduates			Intermediates & Matriculates		
Level of Experience	<5 yrs.	15-20 yrs.	> 30 yrs.	<5 yrs.	15-20 yrs.	> 30 yrs.
Mean	12.98	13.84	13.87	12.52	12.96	14.21
	(1)	(2)	(3)	(4)	(5)	(6)
SD	3.37	2.95	3.21	2.77	2.54	2.89
Combined Mean (Edn.)	Graduates- 13.56			Intermediates-13.23		
Combined Mean (Exp.)	<5 yrs.-12.75		15-20 yrs.-13.40		> 30 yrs.-14.04	
Significant mean differences inTukey's HSD Test:						
Level of Education	Not significant					
Level of Experience	1 vs.2; 1vs.3; 4vs.6; 5vs.6					

Note:- * <.05; ** p<.01

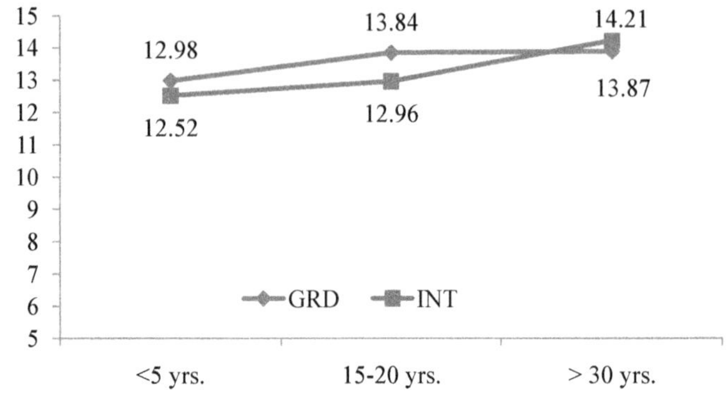

Figure 19a. Fairness (TE) of women teachers compared for level of Education

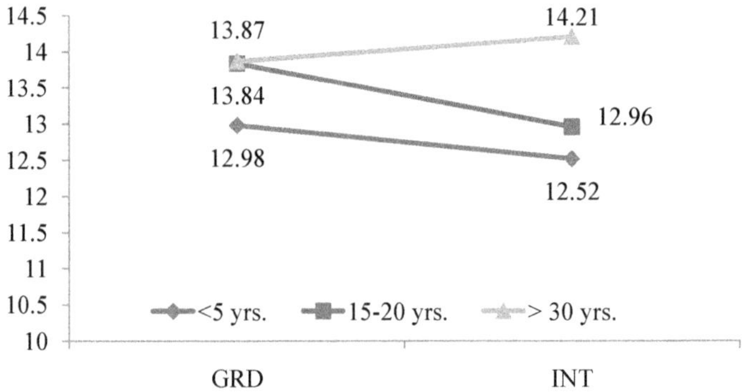

Figure 19b. Fairness (TE) of women teachers compared for level of Experience

The results of two-way ANOVA and Tukey's HSD test for the variable of personal concern are reported in Table 23 and the graphs representing the group means are presented in Figures 20a and 20b. It is observed in the results that the main effect of only the level of experience [F (2, 414) = 27.84, p <.01] is significant and the main effect of level of education and the interaction effect are not significant. The results of Tukey's test also point out that the experience of the teacher towards the later part of their service career make them more concerned about the students notwithstanding their educational qualification.

Table 23
Results of Two way ANOVA (2: Level of Education X 3: Level of Experience) and Tukey's HSD test for Personal Concern (TE) of women teachers

Source	SS		df		MS		F
Level of Education (A)	36.01		1		36.01		3.51
Level of Experience (B)	571.28		2		285.64		27.84**
AXB	90.70		2		45.35		3.42
Error	4247.64		414		10.26		
Level of Education	Graduates & Post Graduates			Intermediates & Matriculates			
Level of Experience	<5 yrs.	15-20 yrs.	> 30 yrs.	<5 yrs.	15-20 yrs.	> 30 yrs.	
Mean	13.07	16.44	16.96	13.29	15.91	15.97	
	(1)	(2)	(3)	(4)	(5)	(6)	
SD	2.26	3.76	3.24	3.19	2.95	3.33	
Combined Mean (Edn.)	Graduates- 15.49			Intermediates-15.06			
Combined Mean (Exp.)	<5 yrs.-13.18		15-20 yrs.-16.18		> 30 yrs.-16.47		
Significant mean differences inTukey's HSD Test:							
Level of Education	Not significant						
Level of Experience	1 vs.2; 1vs.3; 4vs.5; 5vs.6						

Note:- * <.05; ** p<.01

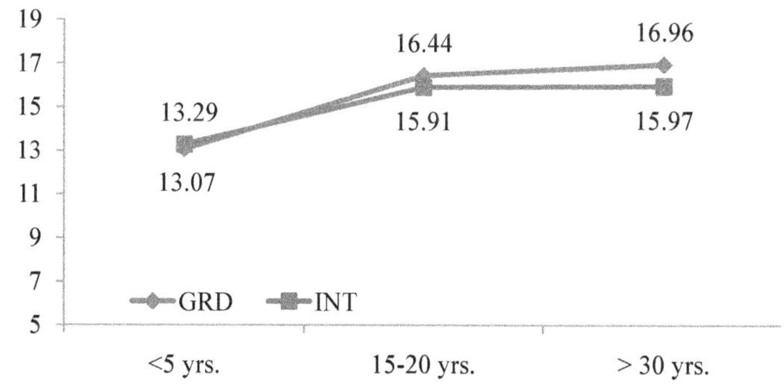

Figure 20a. Personal Concern (TE) of women teachers compared for level of Education

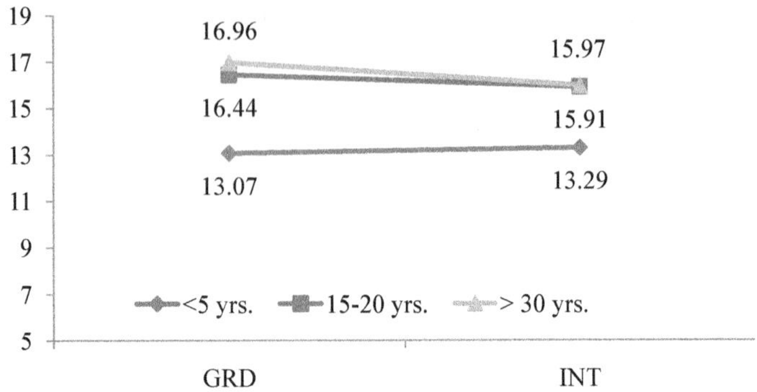

Figure 20b. Personal Concern (TE) of women teachers compared for level of Experience

The results of two-way ANOVA and Tukey's HSD test for the variable of sense of belonging are reported in Table 24 and the graphs representing the group means are presented in Figures 21a and 21b. It is observed in the results that the main effect of both level of education [F (1, 414) = 13.22, p <.01] and the level of experience [F (2, 414) = 63.65, p <.01], including the interaction effect [F (2, 414) = 7.18, p <.01] are significant. Very typical result is observed about this variable. When no differences in belongingness of intermediate teachers were observed during both early and later part of their service career, significant difference was observed during the middle period of their service career. Such differences can only be attributed to some factors in their service conditions which may be related to the promotional prospects in their career. On the other hand, experience has shown consistent contributions to the sense of belongingness of the teachers.

Table 24

Results of Two way ANOVA (2: Level of Education X 3: Level of Experience) and Tukey's HSD test for Sense of Belonging (TE) of women teachers

Source	SS	df	MS	F	
Level of Education (A)	110.92	1	110.92	13.22**	
Level of Experience (B)	1068.05	2	534.02	63.65**	
AXB	120.48	2	60.24	7.18**	
Error	3473.46	414	8.39		
Level of Education	Graduates & Post Graduates			Intermediates & Matriculates	
Level of Experience	<5 yrs.	15-20 yrs.	> 30 yrs.	<5 yrs.	15-20 yrs.	> 30 yrs.
Mean	12.17	15.63	15.91	11.96	13.39	15.37
	(1)	(2)	(3)	(4)	(5)	(6)
SD	3.07	3.11	2.89	2.54	3.15	3.06
Combined Mean (Edn.)	Graduates- 14.57			Intermediates-13.57		
Combined Mean (Exp.)	<5 yrs.-12.07		15-20 yrs.-14.51		> 30 yrs.-15.64	
Significant mean differences inTukey's HSD Test:						
Level of Education	2vs.5					
Level of Experience	1 vs.2; 1vs.3; 4vs.5; 5vs.6; 4vs.6					

Note:- * <.05; ** p<.01

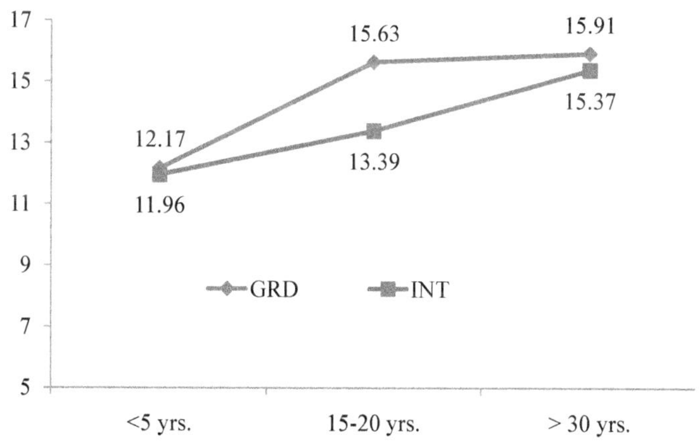

Figure 21a. Sense of Belonging (TE) of women teachers compared for level of Education

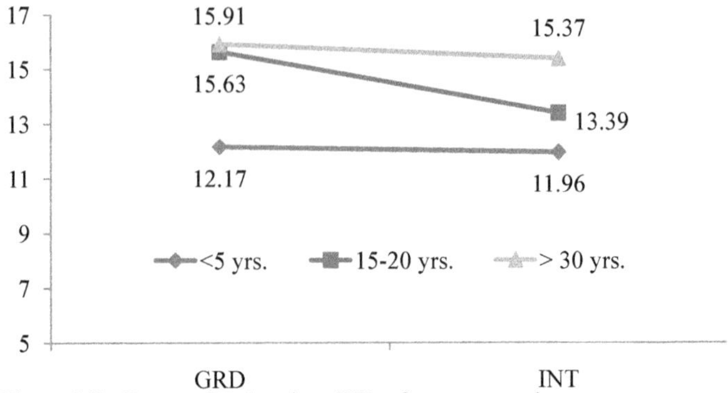

Figure 21b. Sense of Belonging (TE) of women teachers compared for level of Experience

The results of two-way ANOVA and Tukey's HSD test for the variable of respect for students are reported in Table 25 and the graphs representing the group means are presented in Figures 22a and 22b. It is observed in the results that the main effect of both level of education [F (1, 414) = 9.46, p <.01] and the level of experience [F (2, 414) = 77.12, p <.01] are significant while the interaction effect is not significant. The results of Tukey's HSD test point out that during early and later part of the service career, there are no differences in respect for students but in the middle of the service career, significant difference is there in respect for students, that too in favor of the intermediate teachers. Similar results were also found about sense of belongingness variable but that was in favor of graduate teachers. Such typical findings should have to be something related to the service conditions of the teacher which cannot be explained under the scope of the present study. Hence, further observations need to be taken up in future research relating to the service conditions of the teachers so that these discrepant results can be appropriately explained. However, results of Tukey's test very clearly point to the fact that experiences of teachers consistently help them to be more respectful to students.

Table 25

Results of Two way ANOVA (2: Level of Education X 3: Level of Experience) and Tukey's HSD test for Respect for Students (TE) of women teachers

Source	SS	df	MS	F
Level of Education (A)	51.56	1	51.56	9.46**
Level of Experience (B)	840.61	2	420.30	77.12**
AXB	25.94	2	12.97	2.38
Error	2256.30	414	5.45	

Level of Education	Graduates & Post Graduates			Intermediates & Matriculates		
Level of Experience	<5 yrs.	15-20 yrs.	> 30 yrs.	<5 yrs.	15-20 yrs.	> 30 yrs.
Mean	8.45	11.36	14.15	9.12	13.44	14.16
	(1)	(2)	(3)	(4)	(5)	(6)
SD	1.17	1.91	1.45	2.03	2.17	2.34

Combined Mean (Edn.)	Graduates- 11.32	Intermediates-12.24	
Combined Mean (Exp.)	<5 yrs.-8.79	15-20 yrs.-12.40	> 30 yrs.-14.15

Significant mean differences inTukey's HSD Test:

Level of Education	2vs.5
Level of Experience	1 vs.2; 1vs.3; 2 vs.3; 4vs.5; 4vs.6

Note:- * <.05; ** p<.01

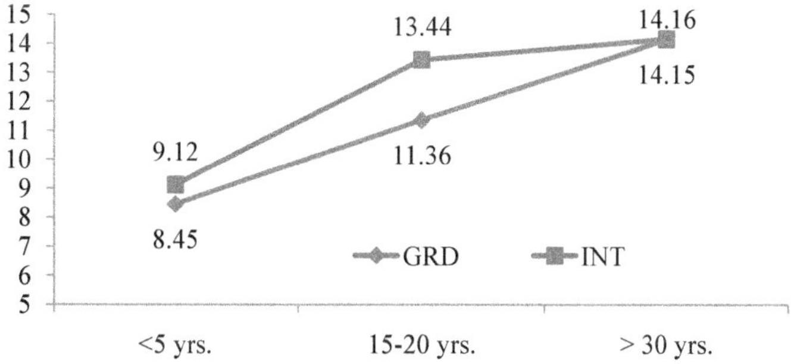

Figure 22a. Respect for Students (TE) of women teachers compared for level of Education

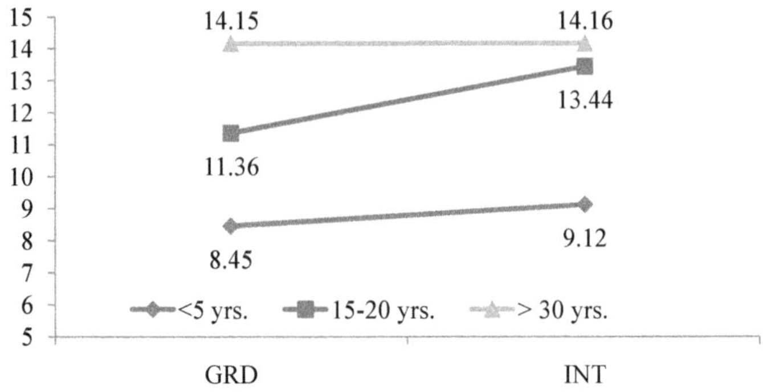

Figure 22b. Respect for Students (TE) of women teachers compared for level of Experience

The results of two-way ANOVA and Tukey's HSD test for the variable of teachers' forgiving are reported in Table 26 and the graphs representing the group means are presented in Figures 23a and 23b. It is observed in the results that the main effect of both level of education [F (1, 414) = 4.41, p <.05] and the level of experience [F (2, 414) = 32.58, p <.01] are significant while the interaction effect is not significant. Tests of Tukey's multiple comparisons shows that while there is no significant difference in forgiveness between intermediate and graduate teachers during early and middle part of their service career, graduate teachers are more forgiving during later part of their service career. On the other hand, with increasing experience, both graduate and intermediate teachers become more and more forgiving.

Table 26
Results of Two way ANOVA (2: Level of Education X 3: Level of Experience) and Tukey's HSD test for Forgiving (TE) of women teachers

Source	SS		df	MS		F
Level of Education (A)	44.67		1	44.67		4.41*
Level of Experience (B)	660.07		2	330.04		32.58**
AXB	44.38		2	22.19		2.19
Error	4193.82		414	10.13		
Level of Education	Graduates & Post Graduates			Intermediates & Matriculates		
Level of Experience	<5 yrs.	15-20 yrs.	> 30 yrs.	<5 yrs.	15-20 yrs.	> 30 yrs.
Mean	12.65 (1)	15.11 (2)	16.23 (3)	11.96 (4)	14.57 (5)	14.69 (6)
SD	3.17	2.39	2.34	2.56	2.36	2.67
Combined Mean (Edn.)	Graduates- 14.66			Intermediates-13.74		
Combined Mean (Exp.)	<5 yrs.-12.31		15-20 yrs.-14.84		> 30 yrs.-15.46	
Significant mean differences inTukey's HSD Test:						
Level of Education	3vs.6					
Level of Experience	1 vs.2; 1vs.3; 2 vs.3; 4vs.5; 4vs.6					

Note:- * <.05; ** p<.01

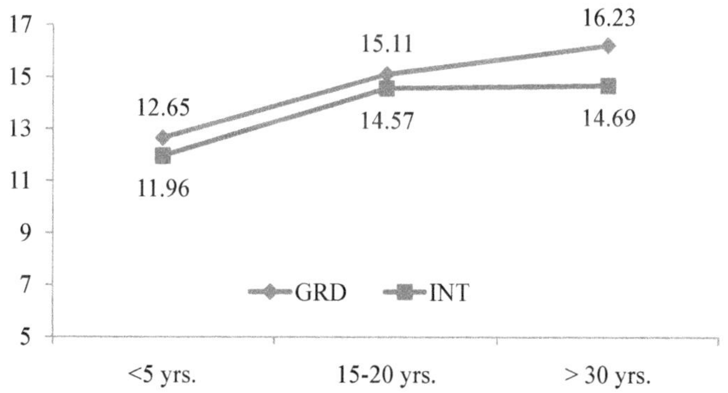

Figure 23a. Forgiving Students (TE) of women teachers compared for level of Education

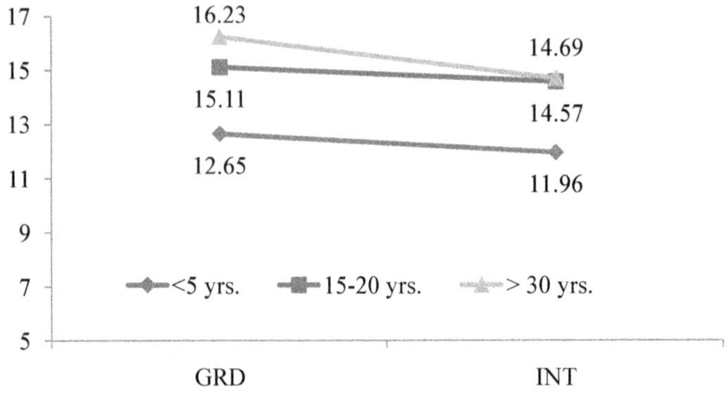

Figure 23b. Forgiving Students (TE) of women teachers compared for level of Experience

Finally, about admitting mistakes, the results of two-way ANOVA and Tukey's HSD test are reported in Table 27 and the graphs representing the group means are presented in Figures 24a and 24b. It is observed in the results that the main effect of only the level of experience [F (2, 414) = 32.58, p <.01] is significant while the main effect of level of education and interaction effects are not significant. The Tukey's HSD test point out that the genuineness of admitting mistakes consistently improve among the women teachers with their increasing experience.

Table 27

Results of Two way ANOVA (2: Level of Education X 3: Level of Experience) and Tukey's HSD test for Admitting mistakes (TE) of women teachers

Source	SS	df	MS	F		
Level of Education (A)	13.68	1	13.68	3.28		
Level of Experience (B)	1397.37	2	698.68	167.55**		
AXB	18.26	2	9.13	2.19		
Error	1726.38	414	4.17			
Level of Education	Graduates & Post Graduates			Intermediates & Matriculates		
Level of Experience	<5 yrs.	15-20 yrs.	> 30 yrs.	<5 yrs.	15-20 yrs.	> 30 yrs.
Mean	7.39	10.65	13.12	8.36	10.67	12.94
	(1)	(2)	(3)	(4)	(5)	(6)
SD	1.45	2.39	2.51	2.07	2.66	2.54
Combined Mean (Edn.)	Graduates- 10.39			Intermediates-10.66		
Combined Mean (Exp.)	<5 yrs.-7.88		15-20 yrs.-10.66		> 30 yrs.-13.03	
Significant mean differences inTukey's HSD Test:						
Level of Education	Not significant					
Level of Experience	1 vs.2; 1vs.3; 2 vs.3; 4vs.5; 4vs.6; 5vs.6					

Note:- * <.05; ** p<.01

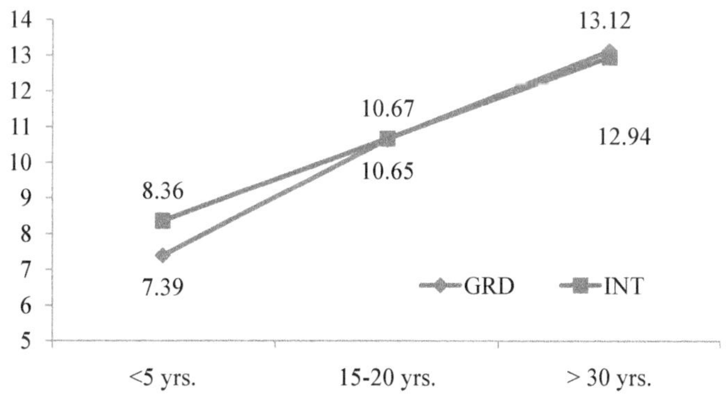

Figure 24a. Admitting mistakes (TE) of women teachers compared for level of Education

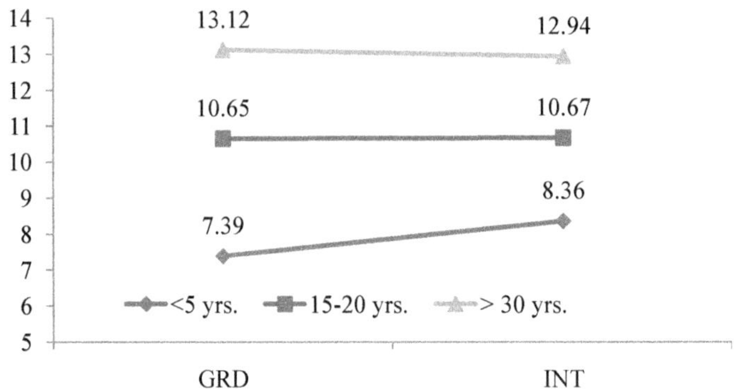

Figure 24b. Admitting mistakes (TE) of women teachers compared for level of Experience

Summary of the findings. Group differences in teacher effectiveness among the women primary teachers in Odisha in respect of their educational qualification and experience were examined following a factorial design. The results pointed out that experience is a predominant factor contributing to teacher effectiveness as significant main effects of experience were observed for each of the ten Walker's attributes of teacher effectiveness. Further, in respect of each of the variables, high F-values clearly establish the significance of teachers' experience in developing their effectiveness as teachers. On the other hand, level of education of the teachers is not found to be so potent a factor for teacher effectiveness in comparison to experience. When the main effects of only six out of the ten teacher effectiveness variables are found significant, all of them have very low F-values excepting the variable of creativity. Further also interaction effects between level of education and level of experience are significant for only three of the ten teacher effectiveness variables and the interaction F-values are very small which suggest that level of education and level of experience have a weak bonding in promoting teacher effectiveness. Hence, arising from the results of the study, it may be suggested to the primary school authority in Odisha to help providing substantial and qualitative experiences to the women primary teachers through awareness campaigns, counseling programs and in-service training schedules so that they become more effective teachers.

Regression Analyses

In order to explain the intricate relationships among psychosocial attributes and teacher effectiveness, multiple regression analyses were carried out to examine how each of the teacher effectiveness variables was predicted by the psychosocial attributes of the teachers. The data of all the 420 subjects were entered into the analyses. The results of multiple regression for significant beta value are presented in Table 28 a, and 28 b. Similarly, in order to examine the relationship among psychological capital and teacher effectiveness, multiple regression analyses were carried out and the results of multiple regression for significant beta values are presented in Table 29 a and 29 b. The summary of the results are as follows.

(i) Each of the teacher effectiveness variables was significantly predicted by 3 or 4 psychosocial attributes. Preparedness was significantly predicted by self-image, locus of control, sensitivity profile and flow mindset and 19% (Table 28 a) of the total variances in teachers' preparedness is explained by these four factors. Hence, it appears from the results of the study that there are also factors other than the psychosocial attributes which influence the classroom preparedness of the women teachers. With respect to Psychological Capital, preparedness is found to have been significantly predicted by self-efficacy, hope and optimism. These three PsyCaps variables explained 24% (Table 29a) of the variances in the teacher effectiveness. Hence, it may be said that PsyCap is a more significant predictor of teacher effectiveness than the psychosocial attributes. However, even though we have not gone for a hierarchical regression analyses, the results of multiple regressions clearly point out that both psychosocial attributes and PsyCap taken together are prominent factors of teacher effectiveness on preparedness.

(ii) The positivity as teacher effectiveness is significantly predicted by four of the psychosocial attributes namely; listening profile, empathetic ability, sensitivity profile and sense of humor. These attributes account for 27% (Table 28a) of variances in the positivity of the teachers. Hence, psychosocial attributes are very important sources of positivity among the teachers resulting in teacher effectiveness. On the other hand 27% (29a) of the variances in teachers' positivity are also explained by three of the PsyCap variables namely; hope, optimism, and resilience. Thus, taken together, psychosocial attributes and PsyCap of the teachers are significant sources of their positivity and thus, teacher effectiveness.

(iii) Teachers' high expectations about students are found to have been significantly predicted by three of psychosocial attributes namely; locus of control, flow mindset, and listening profile. These are also very strong predictors as they explain 32% (Table 28a) of the variances in teachers' expectations about students. Likewise, hope and optimism as PsyCap variables explain 33% (Table 29a) of the variances in high expectations of teachers for students. Hence, it may be said that taken together, psychosocial attributes and PsyCap variables are very significant sources of teacher effectiveness due to teachers' high expectation of students.

(iv) Similarly, teachers' creativity in classroom teaching is significantly predicted by four psychosocial attributes namely; locus of control, listening profile, sensitivity profile and superstition of which superstition is negatively related to creativity. However, 30% (Table 28a) in the variances of creativity are explained by these four psychosocial attributes of the teachers. On the other hand, self-efficacy, hope and optimism as PsyCap are found to have been explained 28% (Table 29a) of the variances in creativity. Hence, it is clear from the findings that both psychosocial attributes and PsyCap are significant sources of teacher effectiveness on creativity in teaching.

(v) Teachers' attribute of fairness is found to have been significantly predicted by ethical and moral values, empathetic ability, and self-image. It is observed that 29% (Table 28a) of variances in fairness attribute are explained by the above psychosocial attributes. Similarly, self-efficacy and optimism as

PsyCap variables have significantly predicted the fairness attribute of the teachers and these two PsyCap variables explained 27% of the variances in the fairness attribute. Hence, it may also be concluded that both psychosocial attributes and PsyCap variables are highly significant sources of teacher effectiveness on fairness attribute.

(vi) Personal concern of the teachers about students is significantly predicted by four of the psychosocial variables namely; self-image, listening profile, sensitivity profile, and sense of humor. These factors explained 25% (Table 28b) of the variances in the personal concern of the teachers. On the other hand, two of the PsyCap variables namely; self-efficacy and optimism have significantly explained 27% (Table 29b) of the variances in personal concern of the teachers. Hence, the findings suggest that both psychosocial attributes and PsyCap are significant sources of teacher effectiveness on personal concern.

(vii) The teacher sense of belonging is significantly predicted by three of the psychosocial attributes namely; self-image, sensitivity profile, and ethical and moral values. These factors predicted 29% (Table 28b) of the variances in belongingness of the teachers. Similarly, three of the PsyCap variables namely; hope, optimism, and resilience significantly predicted the belongingness of the teachers and these attributes explained 28% (Table 29b) of variances in belongingness. Hence, it may be concluded that both psychosocial attributes and PsyCap of the teachers are important sources of teacher effectiveness in sense of belonging.

(viii) Teachers respect for students is found to be significantly predicted by four of the psychosocial attributes namely; punishing behavior, empathetic ability, listening profile, and sense of humor of which punishing behavior is negatively correlated with teachers' sense of respect for students. These factors explained 28% (Table 28b) of the variances in teachers' sense of respect. Similarly, two of the PsyCap measures namely; hope and optimism significantly predicted teachers' sense of respect for the students and accounted for 20% (Table 29b) of the variances. Hence, it may be concluded that both psychosocial attributes and PsyCap of the teachers are important sources of teacher effectiveness in determining teachers' sense of respect for the students.

(ix) Forgiving as a teacher effectiveness skill is found to be significantly predicted by four of the psychosocial attributes namely; empathetic ability, listening profile, sense of humor and punishing behavior of which punishing behavior is found to be negatively correlated with forgiving. The variance explained by these factors is 25% (Table 28b). Similarly, hope and optimism are the two PsyCap measures which significantly predicted the forgiving behavior of the teachers and together they explained 18% of the variances in the forgiving behavior of the teachers.

Hence, it is also concluded that both psychosocial attributes and PsyCap of the teachers are important sources of forgiveness behavior of the teachers.

(x) Finally, sensitivity profile, sense of humor and self image successfully predicted the attitude of the teachers in admitting their own mistakes. These factors explained 19% of the variances in admitting mistakes. On the other hand, optimism and resilience as PsyCap variables significantly predicted the attitude of admitting mistakes and together explained 17% of the variances. Hence, it is also concluded that both psychosocial attributes and PsyCap of the teachers are important sources of teacher effectiveness in determining their attitude for admitting mistakes.

Table 28 a

Multiple regression analyses with the Psychosocial Attributes Regressed on Teacher Effectiveness

Factor	Predictor	Beta	R^2	Adjusted R^2
Prepared	Self-image	.22**		
	Locus of control (Int)	.20**		
	Sensitivity profile	.26**		
	Flow mindset	25**	.19	.18
Positive	Listening profile	.27**		
	Empathetic ability	.24**		
	Sensitivity profile	.31**		
	Sense of humor	22**	.27	.23
Hold high expectations	Locus of control (int.)	18**		
	Mindset (Flow)	23**		
	Listening profile	26**	.32	.30
Creative	Locus of control (int.)	29**		
	Listening profile	21**		
	Sensitivity profile	24**		
	Superstition	-.28**	.30	.27
Fair	Ethical / moral values	.32**		
	Empathetic ability	.27**		
	self-Image	.30**	.29	.27

Note:- * <.05; ** p<.01

Table 28 b

Multiple regression analyses with the Psychosocial Attributes Regressed on Teacher Effectiveness

	Predictor	Beta	R^2	Adjusted R^2
Personal Concern	self-Image	.16**		
	Listening profile	.32**		
	Sensitivity profile	.27**		
	Sense of humor	.26**	.25	.22
Sense of belonging	self-Image	.19**		
	Sensitivity profile	.30**		
	Ethical / moral values	.32**	.29	.27
Respect for students	Punishing behavior	.34**		
	Empathetic ability	.31**		
	Listening profile	.29**		
	Sense of humor	.23**	.28	.26
Forgiving	Empathetic ability	.21**		
	Listening profile	.27**		
	Sense of humor	.33**		
	Punishing behavior	.31**	.25	.24
Admitting mistakes	Sensitivity profile	.19**		
	Sense of humor	.22**		
	self-Image	.16**	.19	.17

Note:- * <.05; ** p<.01

Table 29a

Multiple regression analyses with the PSYCAP Attributes Regressed on Teacher Effectiveness

Factor	Predictor	Beta	R^2	Adjusted R^2
Prepared	Self-efficacy	.32**		
	Hope	.21**		
	Optimism	.25**	.24	.20
Positive	Hope	.34**		
	Optimism	.31**		
	Resilience	.27**	.27	.25
Hold high expectations	Hope	.35**		
	Optimism	.35**	.33	.31
Creative	Self-efficacy	.28**		
	Hope	.24**		
	Optimism	.31**	.28	.25
Fair	Self-efficacy	.26**		
	Optimism	.29**	.27	.25

Note:- * <.05; ** p<.01

Table 29 b
Multiple regression analyses with the PSYCAP Attributes Regressed on Teacher Effectiveness

Factor	Predictor	Beta	R^2	Adjusted R^2
Personal Concern	self-efficacy	.29**		
	Optimism	.27**	.27	.25
Sense of belonging	Hope	.31**		
	Optimism	.30**		
	Resilience	.26**	.28	.26
Respect for students	Hope	.24**		
	Optimism	.22**	.20	.19
Forgiving	Hope	.17**		
	Optimism	.23**	.18	.16
Admitting mistakes	Optimism	.22**		
	Resilience	.16**	.17	.14

Summary of the findings.

(i) Each of the teacher effectiveness variables was significantly predicted by 3 or 4 psychosocial attributes.

(ii) Preparedness and admitting mistakes were least predicted (19%) where as holding high expectations (32%), creativity (30%), fairness (29%), sense of belonging (29%) and respect for students (28%) were most predicted by the psychosocial attributes. Listening profile, empathetic ability, sense of humor, and sensitivity profile are found to have maximum impact on different teacher effectiveness variables.

(iii) Superstition and punishing behavior are found to have negative impacts on teacher effectiveness

(iv) Each of the teacher effectiveness variables was significantly predicted by 2 or 3 PsyCap variables.

(v) Holding high expectations (33%), creativity, belongingness (28%), fairness (27%) and positiveness (27%) are highly predicted teacher effectiveness variables by PsyCap.

(vi) Forgiveness (18%) and admitting mistakes (17%) are least predicted teacher effectiveness variables by PsyCap.

(vii) There is no negative impact of PSYCAP on any of the teacher effectiveness variables

Conclusion

The study was carried out with three major objectives: (i) to describe the state of affairs of women primary school teachers in Odisha in respect of their teacher relevant psychosocial attributes, psychological capital, and teacher effectiveness; (ii) to explain the group differences in respect of all those variables arising from their level of education and level of experience; and (iii) to examine the contributions of psychosocial attributes and PsyCap variables to teacher effectiveness. First of all, relating to the psychosocial attributes supposed to be influencing the teacher effectiveness; the findings have pointed out that while in some of the psychosocial attributes like empathetic ability, listening profile, sensitivity profile, and ethical and moral values, women primary teachers in Odisha are very good, in some others like self image, internal locus of control, and superstition (more superstitious), they are poor with reference to the Chatopadhyay's norm. Further, high values of standard deviations in respect of some of the psychosocial attributes like sensitivity profile, sense of humor, punishing behavior and flow mindset pointed to the fact that there are wide differences among the teachers with respect to these variables. Hence, the overall picture is that the women primary teachers of Odisha are not equipped with all the psychosocial attributes to prove themselves as effective teachers and hence, steps need to be taken to help them improve in deficit areas of their psychological attributes.

The sample used in the present study constituted six groups of teachers varying in their level of education and level of experience. Hence, the second objective of the study was to examine the group differences to know whether education and experience are relevant variables influencing psychosocial attributes of the teachers. Level of education is found to have impact on four of the attributes, i.e., self-image, internal locus of control, empathetic ability, and flow mindset, while for other six psychosocial attributes, level of education is not found to have any impact. On the other hand, excepting superstition, level of experience is found to have impact on all the other nine psychosocial attributes of the teachers. Hence, it was concluded from the study that experience is more important a factor to help the development of the desired psychosocial attributes among the teachers than level of education.

Relevant with studies in the research literature, psychological capital such as self-efficacy, hope, optimism, and resilience of the women primary teachers were also assessed to provide a general idea about their position on these variables. The results pointed out that the teachers are not very good in any of these PsyCap variables. Rather, they may be said to have a below average level in each of these skills. The values of standard deviations are also not high which pointed to the fact that there are no wide differences among the women primary teachers with respect to the PsyCap variables. However, group comparisons were carried out to examine the impact of the level of education and level of experience of the teachers on each of these PsyCap variables. The results pointed out that both level of education and level of experience have significant impact on the development of each of these PsyCap variables of the teachers. Hence, it is suggested that the administration should take note of this fact and develop programs to help the teachers improve their PsyCap skills in order to bring more effectiveness in their teaching.

The variables measuring the teacher effectiveness were also assessed for the women primary teachers of Odisha. In some of the variables like personal concern, sense of belonging, and forgiving, the teachers were found to be good, while in variables like creativity, respect for students, and admitting mistakes, they are found to be poor. However, in other variables like preparedness for the class, positive attitude, holding high expectations for the students, and fairness, they are found to be in average. On the other hand, low values of standard deviations for each of the variables point to the fact that there are not wide differences among the teachers with respect to teacher effectiveness. Group comparisons were also carried out to know the impact of level of education and level of experience on teacher effectiveness. Level of experience is again found to be the most significant source of teacher effectiveness as each of the 10 teacher effectiveness measures is found to be influenced positively by the teacher experience. On the other hand, six of the teacher effectiveness measures namely; preparedness, positive attitude, creativity, sense of belonging, respect for students and forgiving the students are found to have been impacted by the teachers' level of education. Hence, it is suggested that school administration should take note these facts and develop programs to help the teachers to grow up in their teacher effectiveness skills.

Finally, to examine the intricacies of the relationships among psychosocial variables, PsyCap variables and teacher effectiveness variables, multiple regression analyses were carried out to predict teacher effectiveness from both psychosocial and PsyCap variables. The results multiple regression pointed out that 3 to 4 psychosocial variables in different combinations are significantly predicting each of the teacher effectiveness variables and the range of prediction varied between 19 % and 32%. Superstition is found to be the only variable detrimental to teacher effectiveness. Similarly, 2 to 3 PsyCap variables in different combinations are found to have significantly predicted each of the teacher effectiveness variables. The range of prediction varied between 17% and 33%. Hence, the conclusion derived from the regression analyses has a theoretical significance that both psychosocial attributes and psychological capitals are significant sources of teacher effectiveness. Hence, in order to develop proper teacher effectiveness among the women primary school teachers in Odisha, effort should be made to develop their relevant psychosocial attributes and PsyCap skills.

Implications of the Study

(i) A number of psychological attributes are identified as being influenced by the level of education of the women teachers. This information can be used to develop strategies and programs to help the less educated teachers to improve their desired psychosocial skills. Further, in some of the psychosocial skills, both highly educated and less educated teachers have low scores. Such information may be used for training and counseling the teachers to improve their skills.

(ii) Level of experience is found to have significant influence on all the psychosocial attributes. This information may be used by the school administration to make a fair distribution of experienced teachers in all the schools of Odisha, such that each school has some experienced teachers.

(iii) PsyCap of the women teachers are found to be influenced by both their level of education and level of experience. Such information may be used to understand about the PsyCap of the teachers and thereby develop training and counseling programs for further development of their PsyCap

(iv) Variables of teachers' effectiveness are also found to be influenced by their education and experience. This information may be used to improve the effectiveness of teachers for the benefit of both students and the teachers.

(vi) Finally, some intricate relationships between psychosocial attributes, PsyCap and teacher effectiveness are observed in regression analyses which may used by the future researchers for understanding teacher effectiveness in the perspective of these variables.

Suggestions for Future Research

One limitation of the present study was that the psychosocial attributes and the PsyCap variables are assessed and used as independent of each other because no prior research is available which has factorized the psychosocial attributes (Chatopadhyay's, 2014) with the PsyCap measures. Because of this limitation in the theoretical model about the two constructs, hierarchical regression analyses could not be carried out to examine the combined effects psychosocial attributes and psychological capital on teacher effectiveness. Hence, future research may take note of this limitation and find out the common factors among the measures of psychosocial attributes and PsyCap variables and thereby more precisely explain the relationship of teacher effectiveness variables with those derived factors. Another limitation of the study is that the regression analyses were carried out on the data combined from different groups which have sources of error from between groups. However, in the present study, data were collected from different teachers varying in their level of education and level of experience because our primary interest of the study was to explain the teacher effectiveness of the women primary teachers of Odisha in their diversities. Admitting that the data has limitations for regression analyses, it is suggested for the future researchers to take note of this fact and use data from more homogenous group of teachers to examine the relationships among psychosocial attributes, PsyCap variables and teacher effectiveness variables as confirmatory to the findings of the present research.

References

Abler, D. A. (2002). Relationships of teacher organizational commitment and teacher efficacy to school academic standing and teaching experience. *Dissertation Abstract International*, 63 (10), 3427.

Addison, R., & Brundrett, M. (2008). Motivation and demotivation of teachers in primary schools: The challenge of change. *International Journal of Primary, Elementary and Early Years Education,* 36, 79-94.

Adeyemo, D. A. (2001). Teachers' job satisfaction, job involvement, career and organizational commitments as correlates of student-academic performance. *Nigerian Journal of Applied Psychology.* 6(2), 126-135.

Adeyemo, D. A. (2006). Parental involvement, interest in schooling environment as predictors of academic self-efficacy among fresh secondary school students in Oyo state, Nigeria. *Electronic Journal of Research in Educational Psychology.* 5(1), 163-180.

Adeyinka, T., & Adeniyi, S. O. (2011). Locus of control, interest in schooling and self-efficacy as predictors of academic achievement among junior secondary school students in Osun State, Nigeria. *New Horizon in Education,* 59 (1) 25-27.

Akiri, A. A., & Ugborugbo, N. M. (2009). Teachers' effectiveness and students' academic performance in public secondary schools in Delta state, Nigeria. *Studies on Home and Community Science,* 3 (2), 107-113.

Albert, S. (2010). The psychology of superstition: Is magical thinking hurting or helping you? *International Journal of Science Education,* 12, 13-23.

Alliance for Excellent Education. (2004). *Tapping the potential: Retaining and developing high- quality new teachers.* Report: Washington, DC.

Allington, R. L., & Johnston, P. (2002). *Reading to learn: Lessons from exemplary fourth-grade classrooms.* New York: Guilford.

Allison, L. A., & Hirt, J. B. (2002). Comparing the teaching effectiveness of part-time & full-time clinical nurse faculty. *Nursing Education Perspective*, 25 (5), 238-243.

Altugan, A. S. (2015). The effect of cultural identity on learning. *Social and Behavioral Sciences,* 190, 455-458.

Amandeep, K., & Gurpreet, T. S. (2005). A study of teacher effectiveness in relation to teaching competency. *Recent Researches in Education and Psychology.* 71(6), 137-140.

Anyalewechi, S. (1994). A comparative study of teachers and principals perception of characteristics of effective teachers and factors those are influential in teacher effectiveness. *Dissertation Abstract International,* 55 (4), 806-A.

Aremu, A. O. (2000). *Academic Performance and 5 Factor Inventory.* Ibadan: Stirling-Horden.

Arif, M.S., & Rafi, M.S. (2007). Effects of corporal punishment and psychological treatment on students learning and behavior. *Journal of Theory and Practice in Education, 3(2), 171-180.*

Arigbo, P. O., & Adeogun, T. F. (2018). Effect of punishment on students' academic performance: An empirical study of secondary school students in, Abia state, Nigeria. *International Journal of Applied Research and Technology.* 7(10), 52 – 58.

Auten, Y. (2013).The construct of mindfulness. *Journal of Social Issues,* 56, 1-9.

Avey, J., Reichard, R., Luthans, F., & Mhatre, K. (2011). Meta-analysis of the impact of positive psychological capital on employee attitudes, behaviors, and performance. *Human Resource Development Quarterly,* 22, 127-152.

Babu, R., & Fathima, A. (2017). Mental health of women teachers and their professional life stress. *Journal of Humanities and Social Science,* 22 (10), 39-45.

Bacay, S. C. (2006). Humor in the classroom – a dose of laughter won't hurt. *English Journal*, 88 (4), 14-25.

Bajunid, I. A. (2000). Educational management and leadership in Malaysia: The training and professional development of school principals. *Asia-Pacific Journal of Teacher Education and Development*, 3, 49-75.

Bakke, *P. A. L. (*1999*).* Perceptions of characteristics of *effective teachers. Dissertation Abstracts International,* 60(08), 2746-A.

Ballard, *K. J. (*1992*).* A comparison of the *effectiveness* of *teaching and non-teaching principles* in secondary schools. *Dissertation Abstracts International*, 47 (03), 2327-A.

Bandura, A. (1973). Social learning theory of aggression. In J. F. Knutson (Ed.), *The control of aggression: Implication from basic* research (pp.377-404). Chicago: Aldine.

Bandura, A. (1986). From thought to action: Mechanisms of personal agency. *New Zeland Journal of Psychology,* 15 (1), 1-17.

Barrick, M. R., & Mount, M. K. (1991). The big five personality dimensions and job performance: A meta-analysis. *Personnel Psychology*, 44, 1-26.

Baughn, C. A. (1987). An investigation of the utilization of the teacher effectiveness research findings as the standard for teacher evaluation. *Dissretation Abstracts International,* 48 (2), 259.

Bennet, C. K. (1986). The relationship between administrator leadership style and teacher personality variables as a predictor of teacher effectiveness: An exploratory study. *Dissretation Abstracts International,* 47 (6), 1938.

Bergman, P., McLaughlin, M., Bass, M., Pauly, E., & Zellman, G. (1977). *Federal programs supporting educational change: Factors affecting implementation and continuation.* ERIC Document Reproduction Service No. 140432, Santa Monica, CA: RAND.

Bernaus, M., Wilson, A. E., & Gardner, R. (2009). Teachers' motivation, classroom strategy use, students' motivation and second language achievement, *Multilingual Education,* 12, 123-137.

Berry, B., Daughtrey, A., & Wieder, A. (2016). Teacher leadership: Leading the way to effective teaching and learning. *Teaching and Teacher Education*, 27, 308–319.

Beutel, D. (2010). The nature of pedagogic teacher-student interactions: A phenomenographic study. *The Australian Educational Researcher,* 37(2), 77-91.

Biswas, P., Chandra, D. B., & Tinku, D. (1995) A survey on effectiveness of secondary schools teachers in Tripura. *Indian Journal of Psychometry and Education*, 26(1), 17-24.

Blalock, R. E. (1985). The relationship between student achievement as a measure of teaching effectiveness and student's locus of control and self-esteem. *Dissertation Abstracts International*, 6(11), 3289.

Bloom, L. A. (2008). *Classroom management: Creating positive outcomes for all students.* Pearson Education Upper Saddle River: NJ.

Boer, H., & Bosker, R. (2010). Sustainability of teacher expectation bias effects on long-term student performance. *Journal of Educational Psychology*. 102, 168-179.

Bong, M., & Skaalvik, E. (2003). Academic self concept and self efficacy. How different are they really? *Educational Psychology Review*, 15, 1-40.

Branwhite, M.V. (2009). A cross cultural analysis of motivational factors that influence teacher identity. *Electronic Journal of Research in Educational Psychology*, 5 (3), 565-592.

Bread, T. & Hoy, T. C. (2010). Concept mapping, mind mapping and argument mapping: What are the differences and do they matter? *Higher Education*, 14 (3), 112-126.

Brodney, S. B. (1993). The relationship between student achievements, student attitude and student perception of teacher effectiveness. *Dissertation Abstracts International*, 54(8), 2884- A.

Brophy, J. (2006). History of research on classroom management. In C. M. Evertson & C. S. Weinstein (Eds.), *Handbook of classroom management: Research, practice, and contemporary issues*, (pp. 17–43). Mahwah, NJ: Elbrum.

Brown, S., & McIntyre, K. H. (2011). *Making sense of teaching.* Buckingham: Open University Press.

Bruinsma, M., & Jansen, E. P. (2010). Is the motivation to become a teacher related to pre-service teachers' intentions to remain in the profession? *European Journal of Teacher Education*, 33, 185-200.

Bush, C., Caldwell, J., & Shakleford, A. (2016). *Respond to your students with teacher sensitivity.* Charlottesville: University of Virginia Press.

Butler, P. D. (2012). Teachers' listening style and students' academic performance. *Journal of Educational Psychology*, 103 (1), 150-165.

Campbell, R. J., & Neill, S. R. (1994). *Primary teachers at work.* London: Routledge.

Campbell, R. J., Kyriakides, L., Muijs, R. D., & Robinson, W. (2003). Differential teacher effectiveness: Towards a model for research and teacher appraisal. *Oxford Review of Education*, 29 (3), 47-59.

Carbonneau, N., Vallerand, R. J., Fernet, C., & Guay, F. (2008). The role of passion for teaching in intrapersonal and interpersonal outcomes. *Journal of Educational Psychology*, 100 (4), 977-987.

Castle, M. (2003). *Teaching aptitude of the prospective secondary school teachers* Unpublished Master Dissertation, Acharya Nagarjuna University, Andhra Pradesh.

Chatopadhyay, A. (2014). *Psychosocial attributes in teachers' wisdom.* New Delhi: Pustak Mahal Publishers.

Chemers, M. M., Hu, L., & Gracia, B. F. (2001). Academic self-efficacy and first-year college students' performance and adjustment. *Journal of Educational Psychology,* 93 (1), 55-64.

Chen, Jian-xiang . & Yang Jiao-li. (2004). Mental health of female teachers and circumstance in university. *Journal of University of International Business and Economics,* (6), 89-91.

Cheney, D., & Barringer, C. (1995). Teacher competence, student diversity, and staff training for the inclusion of middle school students with emotional and behavioral disorders. *Journal of Emotional and Behavioral Disorders*, 3 (3), 174-182.

Cheung, H.Y. (2006). The measurement of teacher efficacy: Hong Kong primary in-service teachers. *Journal of Education for Teaching*, 32 (4), 435–451.

Chhaya, M. (1974). *An investigation into certain psychological characteristics of ineffective teachers.* Unpublished Doctoral dissertation, Kanpur University, UP, India.

Cicognani, L. (2004). *To punish or discipline? Teachers' attitudes towards the abolition of corporal punishment.* Unpublished Master's Thesis, University of the Witwatersrand, Johannesburg.

Clayson, D. E. (2009). Conceptual and statistical problems of using between-class data in educational research. *Journal of Marketing Education,* 29, 34-38.

Clinton, J., Aston, R., & Koelle, M. (2015). *Investigating the key characteristics of effective teachers: a systematic review.* Melbourne, Australia: Centre for Program Evaluation.

Clotfelter, C. T., Ladd, H. F., & Vigdor, J. L. (2007). Teacher credentials and student achievement in high school: A cross-subject analysis with student fixed effects. *Journal of Human Resources,* 45 (3), 3-11.

Collinson, V., Killeavy, M., & Stephenson, H. J. (1998). *Exemplary teachers: Practicing an ethic of care in England, Ireland, and the United States.*

Paper presented at the annual meeting of the American Educational Research Association, San Diego, CA.

Cosper, B. (1986). An analysis of relationship between teacher effectiveness and teacher planning practice. *Dissretation Abstract International,* 48 (3), 523-A.

Crowley, E. P. (1993). Reflections on a qualitative analysis of mainstreamed behaviorally disordered aggressive adolescents' perceptions of helpful and unhelpful teacher attitudes and behaviors. *Exceptionality,* 4(3), 187-191.

Daly, M. (1990). The relationship of teachers' use of humor in the classroom to immediacy and student learning. *Communication Education,* 39, 46-6.

Danielson, C. (2013). The framework for teaching: Developing highly effective teachers. *English Language Teaching Journal,* 46(1), 71-80.

Dash, K. (2016). *Psychological capital and emotional control of college students.* Unpublished Ph.D. Dissertation, Utkal University, Odisha, India.

Datu, J. A. D., King, R. B., & Valdez, J. P. M. (2018). Psychological capital bolsters motivation, engagement, and achievement: Cross-sectional and longitudinal studies. *The Journal of Positive Psychology,* 13 (3), 260-270.

Deiro, J. A. (1996). *Teaching with heart: Making healthy connections with students.* Thousand Oaks: Corwin Press.

Delso, M. K. (1993). *What good teachers do: A qualitative study approach.* Independent Study, Karnataka University (UGC funded) in the Fifth Survey of Educational Research (1988-1992), Vol. II, NCERT, 1445.

Deshpande, T. (1993). *Evaluation of teaching: A multidimensional approach.* Fifth Survey of Educational Research (1988-1992), Vol. II, NCERT 1445.

Dieter, R. (2000). The use of humor as a teaching tool in the college classrooms. *NACTA Journal,* 44(2), 20-28.

Dika, S. L., & Singh, K. (2002). Applications of social capital in educational literature: A critical synthesis. *Review of Educational Research, 72(1), 31-60.*

Diwan, R. (2010). Small under resourced schools in India: imperatives for quality improvement with reference to RTE Act, 2009. *Edusearch,* 1(2), 8-18.

Donald, L. J. (2014). *Superstitious behavior in classroom teaching*. Thesis for the Degree of Master of Science, University of North Texas.

Duschner, P. (1987) Teacher flexibility in relation to classroom teaching behaviour and perceived teacher-effectiveness, *Dissertation Abstracts International.* 48(6), 1416-1417-A.

Education Week Research Center (2016). *Mindset in the classroom: A National Study of K-12 Teachers.* Annual Report-24, Allington Road, London.

Edwin, S. A. (1991). The perception of principals and the midcareer teachers on teaching effectiveness. *Dissertation Abstracts International*, 52(5), 1589-A.

Egins, D. E. (1987). Teachers perceptions of the impact of the district of Columbia Teacher Center on teaching effectiveness. *Dissertation Abstracts International,* 51(6), 1989-A.

Elawar, M. C., Irwin, T., & Lizarraga, M. S. A. (2007). Looking at teacher identity through self-regulation. *Psicothema,* 22 (2), 293-298.

Elbaz, F. (2007). *Teacher thinking: A study of practical knowledge.* London: Croom Helm.

emotional or behavioral disorders. Journal of Special Educa-

Enzi, S., & Ibrahim, I. (2012), Positive psychological capital (PSYCAP): Conceptual perspective in core basics and requirements for building and preparing. *Journal of Economic and Administrative Sciences,* 18(65), 1-31.

Etebarian, A., Tavakili, S., & Abzari, M. (2012). The relationship between psychological capital and organizational commitment. *African Journal of Business Management,* 6 (14), 57-66.

evaluation on teaching behavior in classrooms for students with

Fagan, L. L. (1996). Relationship between self-concept, self-esteem, anxiety, depression and academic achievement in adolescents. *Journal of Applied Sciences,* 7, 995-1000.

Fielden, C., Kim, L. E., & MacCann, C. (2015). Extraversion. In J. D. Wright (Ed.), *International encyclopedia of the social and behavioral sciences (Second Edition)* (pp. 623–627). Oxford: Elsevier.

Findley, M. J., & Cooper, H. M. (1983). Locus of control and academic achievement: A literature review. *Journal of Personality and Social Psychology*, 44, 419-427.

Finn, L. (2007). *The teachers of 2030: Creating a student-centered profession for the 21st century.* Hillsborough, NC: Center for Teaching Quality.

Fitch-Hauser, M., & Adele, H. M. (2007). Defining the cognitive process of listening: A dream or reality? *Journal of the International Listening Association,* 11, 163-172.

Frenzel, A. C., Becker-Kurz, B., Pekrun, R., Goetz, T., & Lüdtke, O. (2018). Emotion transmission in the classroom revisited: A reciprocal effects model of teacher and student enjoyment. *Journal of Educational Psychology, 110, 628–639.*

Fritz, M. (2004). Characteristics necessary for teacher success in a classroom for students with emotional disabilities. *Journal of Personnel Evaluation in Education,* 17(1), 101-128.

Gao, M., & Liu, Q. (2013). Personality traits of effective teachers represented in the narratives of American and Chinese teachers: A cross-cultural comparison. *International Journal of Humanities and Social Science,* 3(2), 84-95.

Garcia, R., & Cain, K. (2011). Decoding and reading comprehension: A test of the decoding threshold hypothesis. *Journal of Educational Psychology*, 111 (3), 387-401.

Garrison, J., & Liston, D. (2004). *Teaching, learning and loving: Reclaiming passion in educational practice.* New York: Routledge Falmer.

Garza, R. (2007). "She teaches you like if she were your friend": Latino high school students describe attributes of a caring teacher. *Journal of Border Educational Research,* 6 (1), 81-90.

Gaziel, H. (2004). Teacher's personality and students' achievement. *Psychology of Education*, 11, 26-38

Gazit, E. (2013). Teaching mathematics, interest and beauty-walked together and maybe not designed? In S. Phelps-Rosenblatt (Ed.), *Teachers in a changing world—Trends and challenges* (pp.356–389). Raanana: The Open University.

Gero, G. P. (2013). *What drives teachers to improve? The role of teacher mindset in professional learning* (Doctoral Dissertation). Available from ProQuest Dissertations & Theses Global database. (UMI No. 3605669).

Gerstein, J. (2012). *PBL: Project, passion, play based learning.* User Generated Education Blog. San Francisco, CA: Word Press.com.

Glazerman, S. M., Sarah S., Neil, S., & Amy J. (2005). *Design of an impact evaluation of teacher induction programs.* Princeton, NJ: Mathematica Policy Research.

Goe, L., Bell, C., & Little, O. (2008). *Approaches to evaluating teacher effectiveness: A research synthesis.* Washington DC: National Comprehensive Center for teacher Quality.

Goel, S. (1978). *Behavior flow patterns of extrovert and introvert teachers in classroom at secondary level.* Ph.D. Thesis in Education, Meerut University, Meerut.

Gold, Y., & Roth, R. (1993). *Teachers managing stress and preventing burnout.* Washington DC: The Falmer Press.

Goleman, D. (2006). *Emotional Intelligence: Why it can matter more than IQ.* London: Bloomsbury.

Gordon, L. M. (2017, October). *High teacher efficacy as a marker of teacher effectiveness in the domain of classroom management.* Paper presented at the *Annual* Meeting of the California Council on Teacher Education. San Diego, CA.

Gordon, R., Kane, T., & Staiger, D. (2006). *Identifying effective teachers using performance on the job.* New York: The Brookings Institution.

Gorton, B. C. (2003). A transactional model of bullying and victimization. *Social Psychology of Education,* 13(3), 295-311.

Gow, L., & Kember, D. (2007). Conceptions of teaching and their relationship to student learning. *British Journal of Education Psychology*, 63, 20-22

Grewal, S. S. (1976). *Intellectual and personality correlates of teacher effectiveness at the higher secondary school.* Ph. D. Thesis in Education, Punjab University, Chandigarh.

Gupta, B. D. (1988). *Intelligence, adjustment and personality needs of effective teacher in science and arts.* Ph.D. Thesis in Education, Agra University, Agra.

Gupta, S. P. (1995). A correlational study of teachers' job satisfaction and their teaching effectiveness. *The progress of Education*, 69 (10), 207-208.

Guskey, T. R. (1981). Measurement of the responsibility teachers assume for academic successes and failure in the classroom. *Journal of Teacher Education,* 32 (3), 44-51.

Hafen, C. A., Hamre, B. K., Allen, J. P., Bell, C. A., Gitomer, D. H., & Pianta, R. C. (2015).Teaching through interactions in secondary school classrooms: Revisiting the factor structure and practical application of the Classroom Assessment Scoring System. *The Journal of Early Adolescence,* 35, 651-680.

Hameed, A., & Manjusha, M. (2010). Teacher efficacy of secondary school teachers in relation to teaching styles and organizational culture. *Edusearch,* 1(1), 64-70.

Hammond, L. (2007). Race, inequality and educational accountability: The irony of 'No Child Left Behind'. *Race, Ethnicity and Education,* 10 (3), 245-260.

Handayani, S. W. (1985). The relationship between teacher motivation and teacher effectiveness among selected secondary teachers. *Dissertation Abstracts International,* 46 (12), 3550-A.

Hargreaves, D. H. (2012). A self-improving school system in international context. In D. H. Hargreaves (Ed.), *A self-improving school system toward leadership (pp.12-37)*. New York: Basic Books.

Harris, D. N., & Routledge, S. A. (2007). Models and Predictors of Teacher Effectiveness: A Review of the Literature with Lessons from Other Occupations. *Educational Review*, 124(2), 261-268.

Harvey, M., Novicevic, M., & Breland, J. (2007). Global dual-career exploration and the role of hope and curiosity during the process. *Journal of Managerial Psychology,* 42(2), 178–197.

Hattie, J. (2015). The Applicability of Visible Learning to Higher Education. *Scholarship of Teaching and Learning in Psychology*, 1 (1), 79-91.

Hill, M., Gay, L. R., & Baron, A. E. (2015). Teaching and listening skills in multimedia learning. *English Language Teaching,* 8 (12), 117-126.

Hoy, S., & Tarter, P. (2011). An evaluation of the Social and Emotional aspects of learning program: Promoting positive behavior, effective learning and well-being in primary school children. *Oxford Review of Education,* 35 (3), 313-330.

Hudson, P. (2017). Five reasons why listening is important for teachers. *International Teacher Magazine,* 11, 126-138.

Hughes, J. N., Cavell, T. A., & Willson, V. (2001). Further support for the developmental significance of the quality of the teacher–student relationship. *Journal of School Psychology*, 39,289–301.

Ijaiya, N. Y. S. (2008). A Comparative analysis of male and female principals' leadership qualities in selected States of Nigeria. *International journal of Educational Management,* 2 (2), 7 – 13.

Indira, B. (1997). An investigation into teacher effectiveness in relation to work orientation and stress. *Indian Educational Abstract,* (4), 54.

Irving, M. A., & Hudley, C. (2008). Cultural identification and academic achievement among African American males. *Journal of Applied Analysis,* 19 (4), 676-698.

Jesus, L. (2003). Teacher motivation: Theoretical perspectives. *Journal of Educational Psychology,* 104 (3), 150-165.

Jesus, S. N., & Lens, W. (2005). An integrated model for the study of teacher motivation. *Applied Psychology: An International Review,* 54(1), 119-134.

John, O. P., Naumann, L. P., & Soto, C. J. (2008). Paradigm shift to the integrative Big Five trait taxonomy: History, measurement, and conceptual issues. In O. P. John, R. W. Robins, & L. A. Pervin (Eds.), *Handbook of personality: Theory and research* (3rd ed., pp. 114-158). New York, NY: Guilford.

Johns, B. H., & Carr, V. G. (1995). *Techniques for managing verbally aggressive students.* Denver: Love.

Johns, B. H., Crowley, P., & Guetzloe, E. (2005). The central role of teaching social skills. *Focus on Exceptional Children,* 37 (8), 8.

Johnson, K. E. (1992). Learning to teach: Instructional actions and decisions of preservice ESL teachers. *Tesol Quarterly*, 26 (3), 507-535.

Johnson, S. M. (1990). *Teachers at work.* Philadelphia: Basic Books, Inc.

Josephine, U., Joy, D. D., Rose, A., & Utietiang, U. (2015). Superstitious beliefs and academic performance of pupils in early childhood in Ogoja Educational Zone, South Eastern Nigeria. *British Journal of Education,* 3 (11), 54-62.

Judge, T. A., Thoresen, C. J., Bono, J. E., & Patton, G. K. (2013). The job-satisfaction, job performance relationship: A qualitative and quantitative review. *Psychological Bulletin,* 127, 376–407.

Jussim, L. & Harber, K. D. (2005). Teacher expectations and self-fulfilling prophecies: Knowns and unknowns, resolved and unresolved controversies. *Personality and Social Psychology Review*, 9 (2), 131-155.

Juvonen, J. (2006). Sense of belonging, social bonds, and school functioning. In P. A. Alexander & P. H. Winne (Eds.), *Handbook of educational psychology* (2nd ed., pp. 655–674). Mahwah, NJ: Erlbaum.

Kagan, D. M., & Tippins, D. J. (2001). Helping students, teachers attend to student cues. *The Elementary School Journal,* 91(4), 343-356.

Kagathala, A. B. (2002). A study of the effectiveness of teachers of secondary schools in Gujrat. *Journal of Education and Psychology*, 59 (3), 26-33.

Kail, R. (2006). *Advances in child development and behavior*. USA: Academic Press.

Kane, T. J., & Staiger, D. (2008). *Estimating teacher impacts on student achievement: An experimental evaluation.* National Bureau of Economic Research Working Paper No. 14607.

Kane, T. J., Taylor, E. S., Tyler, J. H., & Wooten, A. L. (2011). Identifying effective classroom practices using student achievement data. *The journal of Human Resources,* 46 (3), 587-613.

Kappagoda, S., Othman, H., & De Alwis, G. (2014a). The impact of psychological capital on job performance: Development of a conceptual framework. *European Journal of Business and Management,* 6(14), 143-154.

Kaufman, J. M. (1997). *Characteristics of behavior disorders of children and youth* (6th Ed.). Columbus, OH: Merrill.

Kaufman, J. M., & Wong, K. L. (1991). Effective teachers of students with behavioral disorders: Are generic teaching skills enough? *Behavioral Disorders,* 16(3), 225-237.

Kaul, L. (1974). A factorial study of personality traits of popular teachers. *Indian Educational Review*, 9 (1) 66-78.

Kaur, S. (2008). Occupational stress in relation to teacher effectiveness among secondary school teachers. *Edutracks,* 7, (1), 11-17.

Kerns, C. (2009). Forgiveness at work: Managing the dynamics and reaping the benefits. *Leadership Review*, 9, 80-90.

Kester, V. M. (1994). Factors that affect African-American students' bonding to middle school. *Elementary School Journal*, 95, 63-73.

Khalaf, A. K. (2000). The predictors of chemistry achievement of 12th grade students in secondary schools in the United Arab Emirates. Doctoral dissertation, the Ohio State University, *Dissertation Abstracts International*, Volume, 61-02.

Kim, L. E., & MacCann, C. (2018). Instructor personality matters for student evaluations: Evidence from two subject areas at university. *British Journal of Educational Psychology,* 88 (4)*, 584–60.*

Kirby, P. C., & Teddlie, C. (1989). Development of the reflective teaching instrument. *Journal of Research and Development in Education*, 22(4), 45-50.

Klassen, R., & Tze, V. M. C. (2014). Teachers' self-efficacy, personality, and teaching effectiveness: A meta-analysis. *Educational Research Review*, 12 (6), 59-76.

Krause, K. L., Bochner, S., Duchesne, S., & McMaugh, A. (2010). *Educational psychology: For learning and teaching.* UK: CENGAGE Learning.

Kumar, K. (1999). *A study of teacher effectiveness among scheduled caste and non-scheduled caste teachers in relation to their teaching aptitude and self-concept.* Unpublished doctoral thesis, Punjab University, Chandigarh.

Larrivee, B. (2004). *Assessing teachers' level of reflective practice as a tool for change.* Paper presented at the Third International Conference on Reflective Practice, Gloucester, UK.

Liu, C., Zhao, Y., Tian, X., Zou, G., & Li, P. (2015). Negative life events and school adjustment among Chinese nursing students: The mediating role of psychological capital. *Nurse Education Today*, 35 (6), 754-759.

Long, N. (1996a). The conflict cycle paradigm on how troubled students get teachers out of control. In N. Long, W. C. Morse, & R. G. Newman (Eds.), *Conflict in the classroom: The education of at-risk and troubled students* (5th ed., pp. 244-265). Austin, TX: Pro-E.

Lovorn, M. G. (2008). Humor in the home and in the classroom: the benefits of laughing while we learn. *Journal of Education and Human Development*, 2, (1), 1-12.

Luthans, F., & Youssef, C. M. (2004). Human, social, and now positive psychological capital management. *Organizational Dynamics*, 33, 143–160.

Luthans, F., Luthans, K. W., & Luthans, B. C. (2004). Positive psychological capital: Beyond human and social capital. *Business Horizons,* 47 (1), 45-50.

Luthans, F., Norman, S. M., Avolio, B. J., & Avey, J. B. (2008). The mediating role of psychological capital in the supportive organizational climate-employee performance relationship. *Journal of Organizational Behavior*, 29, 2319–2238.

Luthans, F., Youssef, C. M., & Avolio, B. J. (2007). *Psychological capital.* New York: Oxford University Press.

Makewa, L. N., Role, E., & Genga, J. A. (2011). Teachers' use of humor in teaching and students' rating of their effectiveness. *International Journal of Education*, 3 (2), 353-368.

Male, D. B., & May, D. (1997). Stress, burnout and workload in teachers of children with special education needs. *British Journal of Special Education*, 24(3), 133-140.

Mallam, W. A. (2005). Impact of school-type and sex of the teacher and female students' attitudes toward mathematics in Nigerian secondary schools. *Educational Studies in Mathematics,* 24, 223-229.

Manurung, K., & Mashuri, M. (2017). Implementing interest based instructional materials to minimize EFL learners' speaking skills de-motivating factors. *Theory and Practice in Language Studies*, 7 (10), 132-146.

Marsh, H. W. (1984). Students' evaluations of university teaching: Dimensionality, reliability, validity, potential biases, and utility. *Journal of Educational Psychology,* 76, 707-754.

Masten, A. S., & Wright, M. O. (2010). Resilience over the lifespan: Developmental perspectives on resistance, recovery, and transformation. In J. W. Reich, A. J. Zautra, & J. S. Hall (Eds.), *Handbook of Adult Resilience (*pp. 213-237*)*. New York: The Guilford Press.

Meador, D. (2018). *Why respecting students is essential for teacher effectiveness*. thoughtco.com/respecting-students-is-essential-for-boosting-effectiveness-3194682.

Meadows, P. M. (1997) Teacher Leadership Style and Teacher Effectiveness. *Dissertation Abstracts International*, 58(12), 4555.

Menahem, G. (2011). The impact of community bonding and bridging social capital on educational performance in Israel. *Urban Education*, 46(5), 1100-1130.

Mincucci, S. A. (1988). The relationship of selected teacher biographical characteristics with teacher effectiveness and satisfaction. *Dissertation Abstracts International,* 49(12), 3606-A.

Ming, L., Chou, M., Chin, C., & Wu, H. (2017). The relationship between psychological capital and professional commitment of preschool teachers: The moderating role of working years. *Universal Journal of Educational Research,* 5 (5), 891-900.

More, R. T. (1988). *A study of the relationship between personality, aptitude for teaching and effectiveness of secondary teachers.* Ph.D. Thesis in Education. Nagpur University, Nagpur.

Mortazavi, S., Yazdi, S., & Amini, A. (2012). The role of psychological capital on quality of life and organization performance. *Interdisciplinary Journal of Contemporary Research,* 4(2), 206-217.

Muller, C. (2001). The role of caring in the teacher-student relationship for at-risk students. *Sociological Inquiry,* 71(2), 241-255.

Munir, S., & Sajid, M. (2010). Examining locus of control as a determinant of organizational commitment among university professors in Pakistan. *Journal of Business Studies Quarterly, 1(3), 78-93.*

Murray, H., & Staebler, B. K. (1974) Teacher's locus of control and student achievement gains. *Journal of School Psychology*, 12, 305–309.

Mutha , D. N. (1980). *An attitudinal and personality study of effective teachers.* In M. B. Buch (Ed.) Third survey of research in education, Baroda.

Newa, D. R. (2007). *Teacher effectiveness in relation to work satisfaction, media utilization and attitude towards the use of information and communication technology among secondary school teachers of Nepal.* Unpublished doctoral thesis, Punjab University, Chandigarh.

Newton, X., Hammond, L., Haertel, E., & Thomas, E. (2012). Value-added modeling of teacher effectiveness: An exploration of stability across models and contexts. *Education Policy Analysis,* 18, 138-146.

Nieto, S. (2004). *Affirming diversity: The sociopolitical context of multicultural education.* New York: Allyn & Bacon.

Noerrlinger, G. R. (1987). Student feedback on teacher effectiveness for the purpose of improving instruction. *Dissertation Abstract International*, 49 (1), 22.

Noormohammodi, S. (2014). Teacher reflection and its relation to teacher efficacy and autonomy. *Social and Behavioral Sciences*, 98, 1380-1389.

O'Donnell, A. M., Reeve, J., & Smith, J. K. 2009. *Educational Psychology: Reflection for action*. United States: John Wiley & Sons, Inc.

Olorundare, S. (1998). Superstitious beliefs as constraints in the learning of science. *Nigerian Journal of Guidance and Counseling*, 16 (1), 133-150.

Ormrod, J. E. (2008). *Educational psychology: Developing learners*. (6th Ed.), New Jersey: Pearson Education Inc.

Pajares, F., & Graham, L. (1999). Self-efficacy, motivation constructs, and mathematics performance of entering middle school students. *Contemporary Educational Psychology*, 24, 124-139.

Palmer, R. G. (2011). *Critical thinking dispositions of part time faculty members teaching at the college level.* Unpublished Ph.D. Thesis, Athens, OH: Ohio University.

Palmer, S. M. (1998). *Teacher mindset and skills*. New York: Oxford University Press.

Pandey, M., & Maikhuri, R. (1999). A study of the attitude of effective and ineffective teachers towards teaching profession. *Indian Journal of Psychometry and Education*, 30 (1), 43-46.

Pandit, B., & Surwade, L. (2006). The effect of emotional maturity on teacher effectiveness. *Journal of Educational Track*, 6(1), 74-82.

Pang, V. O. (2005). *Multicultural education: A caring-centered reflective approach*. New York: McGraw Hill.

Pantic, N., & Wubbels, T. (2012). Teachers' moral values and their interpersonal relationships with students and cultural competence. *Teaching and Teacher Education*, 28, 451-460.

Patrick, C. L. (2011). Student evaluations of teaching: Effects of the big five personality traits, grades and the validity hypothesis. *Assessment and Evaluation in Higher Education*, 36, 239-249.

Patrick, J., & Smart, R. M. (1998). An empirical evaluation of teacher effectiveness: The emergence of three critical factors. *Assessment and Evaluation in Higher Education,* 23, 165–178.

Paul, M. (2013). How to create flow on demand: Teacher student relationship. *Success Psychology*, 5 (2), 27-39.

Petersen, P. (2015). That's how much I can do: Children's agency in digital tablet activities in a Swedish preschool environment. *Nordic Journal of Digital Literacy,* 10(3), 145–169.

Peterson, C., & Byron, K. (2008). Exploring the role of hope in job performance. *Journal of Organizational Behavior,* 29 (6), 785-803.

Peterson, C., & Seligman, M. E. P. (2004). *Character strengths and virtues: A handbook and classification.* New York: Oxford University Press.

Peterson, S. J., Luthans, F., Avolio, B. J., & Zang, Z. (2011). Psychological capital and employee performance: A latent growth modeling approach. *Personnel Psychology*, 23 (5), 326-342.

Pianta, R. C., La Paro, K. M., & Hamre, B. K. (2008). *Classroom assessment scoring system manual, K-3.* Baltimore, MD: Paul H. Brookes Publishing Co.

Postlethwaite, T. N. & Wiley, D. E. (2010). *The IEA studies of Science II: Science achievement in 23 countries.* London: Pergamon.

Prakasham, D. (1988). *A study of teacher effectiveness as a function of school organizational climate and teaching competency.* Fifth Survey of Educational Research, 2, 1465-1466.

Pullis, M. (1992). An analysis of the occupational stress of teachers of the behaviorally disordered: Sources, effects, and strategies for coping. *Behavioral Disorders*, 17(3), 191–201.

Punia, V. (2004) *Attitude towards teaching profession and self concept of student teachers of Kerala.* Unpublished M.Ed. dissertation, University of Calicut.

Purser, S. T. R. (1986). The relationship between teacher effectiveness, teacher evaluation, and teacher demographic variables. *Dissertation Abstract International,* 47 (11), 3931-A.

Quandahl, J. E. (2001). The instructional practices of kindergarten teachers: Effects on students' achievement. *Dissertation Abstract International,* 62 (2), 462-A.

Raj, T. (2000). An empirical study of correlates of teacher effectiveness. *The Educational Review*, 107 (1), 6-7.

Rao, K. G. (1995). *A study of teacher effectiveness in relation to creativity and interpersonal relationship.* Ph.D. Thesis, Andhra University, Andhra Pradesh.

Rehman, R., & Ali, H. (2017). Psychological capital as teacher motivator. *Journal of Applied Psychology*, 35, 78-84.

Renninger, K. (2000). Individual interest and its implications for understanding intrinsic motivation. *Motivation and Emotion,* 16(3), 165-185.

Reynolds, D. (2006). World class schools: Some methodological and substantive findings and implications of the international school effectiveness. *Educational Research and Evaluation*, 12(6), 535-560.

Richardson, B. G. (2001). *Working with challenging youth, Lessons learned along the way.* Philadelphia, PA: Brunner-Routledge.

Richardson, B. G., & Shupe, M. J. (2003). The importance of teacher self-awareness in working with students with emotional and behavioral disorders. *Teaching Exceptional Children,* 36, 8-13.

Riolli, L., Savicki, V., & Richards, J. (2012). Psychological capital as a buffer to students' stress. *Psychology*, 3, 1202–120.

Rockoff, J. E., & Speronia, S. (2010). Subjective and objective evaluations of teacher effectiveness. *American Economic Review*, 100 (2): 261-66.

Rodabaugh, C. (2015). Institutional commitment to fairness in college teaching. *New Directions for Teaching and Learning*, 12, 37 - 45.

Rose, J. S., & Medway, F. J. (1993). Measurement of teachers' beliefs in their control over student outcome. *Journal of Educational Research*, 21(3), 185-190.

Rotter, J. B. (1966). Generalized expectancies for internal versus external control of reinforcement. *Psychological Monographs*, 80, 1-28.

Rubie-Davies, C. M. (2008). Teacher beliefs and expectations: Relationships with students learning. In C.M. Rubie-Davies and C. Rawlinson (Eds.), *Challenging thinking about teaching and learning.* NY: Nova Haupagge.

Salmona, M., Partlo, M., Kaczynski, D., & Leonard, S. N. (2015). Developing culturally competent teachers: An international student teaching field experience. *Australian Journal of Teacher Education*, 40(4), 35-53.

Santagata, R. (2005). Practices and beliefs in mistake-handling activities: A video study of Italian and US mathematics lessons. *Teaching and Teacher Education,* 21, 491-508.

Santisi, G., Magnano, P., Hichy, Z., & Ramaci, T. (2014). Metacognitive strategies and work motivation in teachers: An empirical study. *Social and Behavioral Sciences*, 116, 1227-1231.

Saruis, J. B. K. (1989). Comparison of attitude of selected school teachers and principals towards the importance of teacher effectiveness characteristics in conducting teacher evaluation. *Dissertation Abstract International*, 50 (11), 3469-70A.

Scheck, D. C., & Rhodes, G. A. (2001). The relationship between junior high school teachers' rated competence and locus of control. *Education*, 100(3), 243-48.

Schulte, P. D., Slate, R. J., & Onwuegbuzie, J. A. (2008). Effective high school teachers: A mixed investigation. *International Journal of Educational Research*, 47, 351-361.

Schunk, D., & Ertmer, P. (2000). Self-regulation and academic learning: Self-efficacy enhancing interventions. In J. Boekarts, P. Pintrich and M. Zeidner (Eds.) *Handbook of Self-Regulation*. Burlington, MA: Elsevier Academic Press.

Seligman, M. E. P. (1999). Positive Social Science. *Journal of Positive Behavior Intervention*, 1 (3), 20-27.

Seligman, M. E. P. (*2002*). *Authentic happiness: Using the new positive psychology to realize your potential for lasting fulfillment*. New York, NY, US: Free Press.

Seligman, M. E. P. (2007). Coaching and positive psychology. *Australian Psychologist, 42* (4), 266-267.

Selsor, M. K. (2003). Rural and Suburban community college student's perceptions of teaching effectiveness. *Dissertation Abstracts International*, 64(2), 380.

Sergeant, T. & Hannum, E. (2003). *Keeping teachers Happy: Career Satisfaction among Primary School teachers in Rural China.* Paper prepared for the International Association Research Committee on Social Satisfaction and Mobility. New York University, New York City, U.S.A.

Shah, M. (2012). The impact of teachers' collegiality on their organizational commitment in high- and low-achieving secondary schools in Islamabad, Pakistan. *Journal of Studies in Education*, 2 (10), 493-502.

Shamina, E., & Muthas, N. S. (2018). Classroom Management: Implications for teachered preparation programs. *Journal of Humanities and Social Science*, 23 (1), 41-44.

Sharma, S. (2010). *A study of superstitious and non-superstitious B Ed students decision making ability, self confidence, and stress.* Unpublished Ph. D. Dissertation, Institute of Advanced Studies in Education, Chur, Rajstan.

Sharma, U. (1991). Measurement of teacher effectiveness and its relationship with job satisfaction and attitude towards profession. *Trends in Education*, 22 (2), 51-58.

Shumba, O. (1999). Relationship between secondary science teachers' orientation to traditional culture and beliefs concerning science instructional ideology. *Journal of Research in Science Teaching*, 16 (3), 43-51.

Shupe, T. L. (2012). The effect of self-evaluation on teaching behavior in classrooms for students with emotional and behavioral disorders. *The Journal of Special Education,* 35 (3), 161-171

Sikora, D. A. (1997). Observable teacher effectiveness and personality type of family and consumer science teachers. *Dissertation Abstract International*, 59 (7), 2285A.

Simarasl, N., Fayyazi, M., & Arian, G. (2010). Explaining the positive outcomes of psychological factors in the organization. *Journal of Management,* 17, 1-24.

Sin, N. L., & Lyubomirsky, S. (2009). Enhancing well-being and alleviating depressive symptoms with positive psychology interventions: A practice-friendly meta-analysis. *Journal of Clinical Psychology,* 65 (5), 467-487.

Singh, D. (1991). *Creativity and intelligence as correlates of teacher effectiveness of secondary school teachers.* Unpublished doctoral thesis, Punjabi University, Patiala.

Singh, G. (2002). *A comparative study of job satisfaction of teacher educators in relation to their values, attitude towards teaching and teacher effectiveness*. Unpublished doctoral thesis, Punjab University, Chandigarh.

Singh, Om. (2016). A Study on Job related Stress among school teachers in different schools of West Bengal, India. *Eastern Journal of Psychiatry*, 7 (4), 12-17.

Singh, R. S. (1987). *Teaching effectiveness and its correlates at higher secondary stage in eastern UP*. Unpublished doctoral thesis, Gorkhpur University, Gorkhpur, Uttar Pradesh.

Sirvani, H. (2007a). Effects of teacher communication on parents' attitudes and their children's behaviors at schools. *Education,* 128, 34–47.

Slavin, R. E. (2009). *Educational Psychology: Theory and Practice*. 9th Ed., New Jersey: Pearson Education Inc.

Smith, K. E. (1986). Sex-typed occupational roles and self-image among teachers. *Psychological Reports*. 58, 73-74.

Sparks, R., & Lipka, R. P. (1992). Characteristics of master teachers: Personality factors, self-concept, locus of control, and pupil control ideology, *Journal of Personal Evaluation in Education,* 5 (3), 303-311.

Sridhar, Y. N., & Badiei, H. R. (2008). Teacher Efficacy Beliefs: A Comparison of Teachers in India and Iran. *Journal of the Indian Academy of Applied Psychology,* 34, Special Issue, 81-89.

Sultanoff, S. M. (1999). President's column.*Therapeutic Humor*, 13 (4), 2-4.

Sutherland, K. S., & Wehby, J. H. (2001a). The effect of self-

Sutherland, K. S., & Wehby, J. H. (2001a). The effect of self-evaluation on teaching behavior in classrooms for students with emotional and behavioral disorders. *Journal of Special Education*, 35, 161-171.

Talbot, A., & Lumden, B. (2013). On the association between humor and burnout. *International Journal of Humor Research*, 13 (4), 419–428.

Teach for America (TFA) corps (2010). *Maximize our impact on students' achievement.* TEACH FOR AMERICA-Annual Report-2010.

Tirri, K. (2011). *Measuring multiple intelligences and moral sensitivities in education.* Sense Publisher, USA: Boston.

Torok, S. R., McMorris, & W. Lin. (2004). Is humor an appreciated teaching tool? Perceptions of professors' teaching styles and use of humor. *College Teaching*, 52 (1), 14-20.

Totterdell, P., Wood, S., & Wall, T. (2006). An intra-individual test of the demands-control model. *Journal of Occupational and Organizational Psychology,* 79, 63-85.

Tulis, M. (2013). Error management behavior in classrooms: Teachers' responses to student mistakes. *Teaching and Teacher Education,* 33, 56–68.

Ulug, M., Ozden, M. S., & Eryilmaz, A. (2011). The Effects of Teachers' Attitudes on Students' Personality and Performance. *Social and Behavioral Sciences*, 30, 738-742.

Underhill, A. (1991). The role of groups in developing teachers' self-awareness. *English Language Teaching Journal*, 46 (1), 71-79

Varma, J. (2010). *The Principles and Methods of Teaching*. POAB House Publishers. New Delhi. India.

Vijaylaxmi, R., & Mithill, T. (2004). *Mental development in the child and the race: Methods and processes.* 3rd Ed., New York and London: Macmillan.

Walker, R. J. (2008). *Twelve Characteristics of an Effective Teacher*. NC: Lulu Publishing.

Wallace, T. L., Kelcey, B., & Ruzek, E. (2016). What can student perception surveys tell us about teaching? Empirically testing the underlying structure of the tripod student perception survey. *American Educational Research Journal,* 53, 1834–1868.

Wang, J. H., Chen, Y. T., & Hsu, M. H. (2014). A Case Study on Psychological Capital and Teaching Effectiveness in Elementary Schools. *International Journal of Engineering and Technology,* 6 (4), 331-337.

Webber, J., Anderson, T., & Otey, L. (1991).Teacher mindsets for surviving in BD classrooms. *Intervention in School and Clinic*, 26, 288-292.

Weinstein, R. S. (2002). *Reaching higher: The power of expectations in schooling.* Cambridge, MA: Harvard University Press.

Wentzel, K. (1998). Social Relationships and Motivation in Middle School: The Role of Parents, Teachers, and Peers. *Journal of Educational Psychology*, 90, 202-209.

Wilson, S. (1996). Student teacher perceptions of effective teaching: A developmental perspective. *Journal of Education for Teaching*, 22, 181-196.

Wolvin, A. D. (2010). Listening and human communication in the 21st century. In Wolvin (Ed.), *Human communication in the 21st century* (pp.44-56). Malden, MA: Blackwell Publishing Ltd.

Woolfolk, A. (2007). *Educational Psychology*. 10th ed. United States: Pearson Education Inc.

York, K. M. (2014). *Visible learning for teachers*. Abingdon, U.K.: Routledge.

Zhao, Y. (2006). Investigation on mental health of female teachers in universities. *Journal of China Women's College*, 18(4), 56-59.

Zimmerman, B. J. (2000). Attaining self-regulation: A social cognitive perspective. In M. Boekaerts, P.R. Pintrich, & M. Zeidner (Eds.), *Handbook of self-regulation* (pp. 13–39). San Diego, CA: Academic Press.

Appendices

Appendix 1

Chatopadhyay's Scale of Psychosocial Attributes

Instructions: The following are some statements relating to you as a person and a teacher. In respect of your thinking, believe, attitude and conviction, you evaluate yourself on a four-point scale, ranging from 0 to 3. When you strongly disagree with statement, assign a score of '0' and when you strongly agree with the statement; assign a score of '3'. When you think of something in between, assign a score of 1, or 2 as relevant to how much do you agree with the statement. This information will be used only for the purpose of research and it will be totally confidential. Therefore please give your genuine response.

Strongly disagree-0	Disagree-1	Agree-2	Strongly agree-3	Put your score

1	Generally speaking, I think I am a good teacher	
2	When I make plans, I am almost certain that I can make them work.	
3	I feel relaxed when I talk to my students	
4	I enjoy making my students people feel better	
5	I do not discriminate among students because of their caste.	
6	It is important to me to have a lot fun in my class.	
7	Giving extra homework as a punishment only results in the learners hating the subject	
8	I always make sure that my actions never intentionally harm my students even to a small degree.	
9	I believe that black cat crossing the road is a sign of accident.	
10	No matter who the student is, you can significantly change his /her level of intellectual functioning.	
11	I believe in my own abilities	
12	In my case getting what I want has little or nothing to do with luck.	
13	I patiently listen to the problems of my students and give them proper advice.	
14	I can tell when a student is sad even when he or she does not say anything.	
15	I do not have preference for boys over girls.	
16	I tell jokes to students in the class	
17	Efficient teachers have less discipline problems	
18	I am friendly, helpful and welcoming to my students and colleagues	
19	Some numbers are not good for me to begin a work	

20	You always prefer to take academic challenges and try to solve it.	
21	I think I have good teaching abilities and skills.	
22	Getting people to do the right thing depends upon ability	
23	I join with students in the class discussions	
24	It upsets me to see someone being treated disrespectfully.	
25	I treat students from rich and poor families equally.	
26	Sometimes, I engage in some form of physical bodily humor	
27	Corporal punishment is necessary in order to maintain discipline at school	
28	I am trustworthy and loyal to my profession	
29	Tantras can improve the prospect of one's life.	
30	You don't easily give up a problem situation; you always try to fight back.	
31	I have reputation for being an efficient teacher.	
32	There is a direct connection between how hard the students study and the grades they get.	
33	In every class, I spend part of the time listening from the students about their point of view on the topic discussed.	
34	I feel it silly for people to cry out of happiness.	
35	I visit the family of students when they invite me on some occasion.	
36	Sometimes I demonstrate natural phenomenon in humor like letting air out of a balloon to demonstrate air pressure.	
37	Corporal punishment prepares learners to become victims of abuse	
38	I am cheerful and always look at the Brightside of things	
39	Breaking a mirror is a sign of misfortune	
40	You believe that efforts are always the path to mastery.	
41	I feel I am a valuable person.	
42	Many times I feel that I have little influence over the things that happen to me.	
43	I listen to the parents and compliment them when they say something good about their children.	
44	I am not really interested in how other people feel.	
45	I take active part in Students function and enjoy the activities.	
46	I sometimes assign a role playing exercise to students that is humorous.	

47	Detention is an effective way of preventing pupils from misbehaving	
48	I have a religious faith but I respect all religions.	
49	Black magic can cure the incurable diseases	
50	You try to learn from criticisms.	
51	I feel integrated with my colleagues.	
52	Most misfortunes are the result of lack of ability, ignorance, laziness, or all three.	
53	Out of the class, I participate with when they discuss something of their interest.	
54	I do not feel sympathy for people who cause their own illness.	
55	I support the students with special needs.	
56	Sometimes, I make self-disclosure which is embarrassing in my life.	
57	A good teacher is one who does not use corporal punishment to discipline students	
58	I am responsible to my students, colleagues and the school where I work	
59	Thieves can be caught by a Tantric in rounding a cot.	
60	You don't feel threatened from the success of others.	
61	It is easy for me to share and cooperate with others.	
62	Most students don't realize the extent to which their grades are influenced by accidental happenings.	
63	I also listen to my colleagues when they share their problems with me.	
64	When I see someone being taken advantage of, I feel kind of protective towards him/her	
64	I have tender, concerned feelings for people less fortunate than me	
65	I emphasize on students habit of cleanliness.	
66	I role play role-play some character related to the subject in humorous fashion.	
67	Corporal punishment increases aggression in learners	
68	I know thinking good thoughts are important in life.	
69	Evil spirits stay away from home if you hang lemon on the door.	
70	In the face of failure, you escalate your efforts and look for new strategies	
71	I enjoy my interpersonal relations at work.	

72	There's not much use in trying too hard to please people, if they like you, they like you.	
73	Students consider me as a good counselor.	
75	I always like to be friendly with my students.	
76	Sometime, I describe a humor from a cinema or TV serial.	
77	It is morally correct that a student who has done wrong be punished for it	
78	I never think badly of other people.	
79	People can be killed by tetras.	
80	You believe that one can change one's basic level of talent.	

Note: - Below are the item numbers for each of the psychosocial attributes. There will be reverse scoring for some identified items (This part of the schedule is not provided in the teachers' copy).

Self-image	1	11	21	31	41	51	61	71
Locus of Control	2	12	22	32	42	52	62	72
Listening profile	3	13	23	33	43	53	63	73
Empathetic ability	4	14	24	34	44	54	64	74
Sensitivity Profile	5	15	25	35	45	55	65	75
Sense of humor	6	16	26	36	46	56	66	76
Punishing behavior	7	17	27	37	47	57	67	77
Ethical and moral values	8	18	28	38	48	58	68	78
Superstition	9	19	29	39	49	59	69	79
Flow mindset	10	20	30	40	50	60	70	80

Appendix 2

Adult psychological capital scales

Instructions: The following are some statements relating to you as a person and a teacher. In respect of your thinking, believe, attitude and conviction, you evaluate yourself on a four-point scale, ranging from 0 to 3. When you completely disagree with statement, assign a score of '0' and when you completely agree with the statement; assign a score of '3'. When you think of something in between, assign a score of 1, or 2 as relevant to how much do you agree with the statement. This information will be used only for the purpose of research and it will be totally confidential. Therefore please give your genuine response.

Strongly disagree-0	Disagree-1	Agree-2	Strongly agree-3	Put your score

1	I believe what my students' parents tell me.	
2	I can think of many ways to help my students get over their problems.	
3	I tend to bounce back quickly after hard times.	
4	I am competent in designing individualized learning.	
5	I believe my students are competent learners	
6	I feel tired about the various problems my students create in the class.	
7	I can deal with whatever comes in the future.	
8	I always provide alternative explanations to concepts I teach in the class.	
9	I trust my students	
10	I believe as a teacher there are lots of ways to solve any problem	
11	I learn from my mistakes	
12	I control students' disruptive behavior in the class very well.	
13	My students are cooperative during classroom instruction	
14	I always try to meet the goals that I set for myself and my students.	
15	I can come up different ways to lay out my feelings.	
16	I always try to involve parents in school activities.	
17	I am able to get through to the most difficult students	
18	Even when others get discouraged, I know I can find a way to solve the problems in the school.	
19	I can change my behavior to match the situation	
20	I am good at judging students' comprehension in the classroom teaching.	
21	I can do to motivate students who show low interest in school work?	

22	My past experiences have prepared me well for my future as a teacher.	
23	I know when I am good at something.	
24	It gives me pleasure to work with very capable students.	
25	My students' parents are reliable in their commitments	
26	I usually find myself worrying about my career.	
27	When something goes wrong, I can tell if it my fault.	
28	I am open to advice from colleagues.	
29	Students in my classroom can achieve the goals that I set for them.	
30	I am frequently worried about my health.	
31	My friends know they can count on me.	
32	I critically reflect on my learning process.	

Below are the item numbers for each of the PsyCap variables. There will be reverse scoring for some identified items (This part of the schedule is not provided in the teachers' copy).

Optimism	1	5	9	13	17	21	25	29
Hope	2	6	10	14	18	22	26	30
Resilience	3	7	11	15	19	23	27	31
Self-efficacy	4	8	12	16	20	24	28	32

Appendix-3

Teacher Effectiveness Scale

Instructions: The following are some statements relating to your profession as a teacher. In respect of your thinking, believe and attitude, you evaluate yourself on a five-point scale, ranging from 0 to 4. When you strongly disagree with statement, assign a score of '0' and when you strongly agree with the statement; assign a score of '4'. When you think of something in between, assign a score of 1, 2, or 3 as relevant to how much do you agree with the statement. This information will be used only for the purpose of research and it will be totally confidential. Therefore please give your genuine response.

Strongly disagree-0	Disagree-1	Neither agree nor disagree-2	Agree	Strongly agree-4	Put your score

1	Before going to a class you fully prepare about the subject you are going to teach.	
2	You make yourself available to any student when he or she requires your help.	
3	You consistently challenge your students to do their best.	
4	In your class you encourage discussions among the students on the subject being taught.	
5	You believe that you allow equal opportunity and privileges to all students.	
6	You try to connect with all students personally.	
7	You cooperate with the head master and other teachers in the disposal of daily school work.	
8	You behave sisterly / motherly with all your students.	
9	You don't take grudge on a student who you find creating disturbances in the class, but try to change his / her behavior by getting closer.	
10	When you find you have done a mistake, you admit it gracefully.	
11	You regularly prepare your lesson plans and lesson notes.	
12	You communicate with students about their progress.	
13	You believe that any student has immense potentiality.	
14	You always try to use unconventional teaching methods.	
15	You know that all students do not learn in the same way and therefore, you try to address their needs differently.	
16	When you meet the parents or guardians of the students, you behave with them very cordially.	
17	You never do anything against the welfare of the school and the students.	
18	You don't embarrass your students for their mistakes.	

19	Your students very often apologize to you for their wrong behavior.	
20	You apologize for your mistake to your fellow teachers.	
21	You use different teaching aids in the class	
22	You give praise and recognition to your students when they deserve it.	
23	You try to build students' confidence.	
24	You don't discourage when a student comes up with a new idea about something.	
25	You are fair in your assignment of grades to your students.	
26	You give personal time to parents for solution of their child's academic and even otherwise problems.	
27	You have a good relation of friendship and brotherhood with your fellow teachers.	
28	You never discuss or disclose students' private issues or issues relating to their parents.	
29	When you find that a student's wrong behavior is corrected, you verbally appreciate and praise him / her.	
30	You always try to learn from your mistakes.	
31	Very often you use the black board while explaining a concept to the students.	
32	You use strategies to help students act positively toward one another.	
33	You help the students to believe in themselves.	
34	You use modern technology to teach your students.	
35	You don't explicitly demonstrate otherwise behavior to your favorite students.	
36	You regularly visit students' home and discuss with parents about their child.	
37	You give your attention to the cleanliness of the classrooms and school campus.	
38	When you see a student with his / her parents in an outside place, you greet them jovially and talk to them appropriately.	
39	You don't immediately communicate about a student's misbehavior to the headmaster of the school.	
40	You believe that you have not done any mistake during your career as a teacher.	
41	You engage the students in the class from the beginning to the end.	

42	You solve the illogical questions of your students patiently.	
43	You encourage parents about their child's performance.	
44	You try to explain the concept of your teaching using experiences of life.	
45	You have no feeling of caste, creed or gender discrimination.	
46	You share your personal feelings and experiences with students in the class.	
47	You most enjoyably spend your time in the school.	
48	You respond sensitively to the feelings of the students when you find they are hurt.	
49	You like to be most forgiving to your students.	
50	You admit that you do mistakes in some specific kind of tasks.	
51	When students ask questions, you almost always answer them immediately.	
52	You don't hesitate to clarify your doubts with your fellow teachers.	
53	You give examples of great people to encourage your student's motivation.	
54	You use different formats while giving assignments to your students.	
55	You evaluate the answer scripts of the students without any bias.	
56	You take personal interest in students and find out as much as possible about them.	
57	You celebrate the days of function in the school with teachers and students and enjoy them very much.	
58	You believe that all students are equal for you.	
59	You plead for a student's poor performance to allow him / her chance next time.	
60	You encourage students to admit their mistakes because it will help them to improve.	

Below are the item numbers for each of the teacher effectiveness variables. There will be reverse scoring for some identified items (This part of the schedule is not provided in the teachers' copy).

Prepared	1	11	21	31	41	51	Positive	2	12	22	32	42	52
Expectations	3	13	23	33	43	53	Creative	4	14	24	34	44	54
Fair	5	15	25	35	45	55	Concern	6	16	26	36	46	56
Belonging	7	17	27	37	47	57	Respect	8	18	28	38	48	58
Forgiving	9	19	29	39	49	59	Mistakes	10	20	30	40	50	60

CPSIA information can be obtained
at www.ICGtesting.com
Printed in the USA
LVHW081814261122
734044LV00013B/472

9 781805 450191